VGM Opportunities Series

OPPORTUNITIES IN
RESEARCH AND
DEVELOPMENT
CAREERS

Jan Goldberg

Foreword by
Deborah L. Sattley
Research Assistant
Jane Addams College of Social Work

VGM Career Horizons
a division of *NTC Publishing Group*
Lincolnwood, Illinois USA

Cover Photo Credits

Upper left courtesy of the U.S. Institutes of Health; upper right courtesy of DeVry Institutes; lower right courtesy of the Dow Chemical Company; and lower left courtesy of Zenith Electronics Corporation.

Library of Congress Cataloging-in-Publication Data

Goldberg, Jan.
    Opportunities in research and development careers / Jan Goldberg.
        p.   cm. — (VGM opportunities series)
    Includes bibliographical references (p.).
    ISBN 0-8442-4649-2 (alk. paper). — ISBN 0-8442-4650-6 (pbk. : alk.
paper)
    1. Vocational guidance.   2. Research—Vocational guidance.
3. Social sciences—Research—Vocational guidance. I. Title.
II. Series.
HF5381.G5683   1997
331.7′02—dc20   96-27800
                                            CIP

Published by VGM Career Horizons, a division of NTC Publishing Group
4255 West Touhy Avenue
Lincolnwood (Chicago), Illinois 60646-1975, U.S.A.
© 1997 by NTC Publishing Group. All rights reserved.
No part of this book may be reproduced, stored in a retrieval
system, or transmitted in any form or by any means,
electronic, mechanical, photocopying, recording or otherwise,
without prior permission of NTC Publishing Group.
Manufactured in the United States of America.

6 7 8 9 0 VP 9 8 7 6 5 4 3 2 1

CONTENTS

ABOUT THE AUTHOR

Jan Goldberg's investigative spirit and affinity for the printed page have long been part of her. Even before her second birthday, regular visits to the book bindery where her grandfather worked produced a magic of sights and smells that she carries with her to this day.

Childhood was filled with composing poems and stories, reading books, playing library, and searching for answers to questions of all sorts. While a full-time student, Goldberg wrote extensively as part of her job responsibilities in the College of Business Administration at Roosevelt University in Chicago, Illinois. After receiving a degree in elementary education, she was able to extend her love of reading, writing, and researching to her students.

Beginning her career as a poet, Goldberg's work appeared in *Bell's Letters, Complete Woman,* and a number of poetry anthologies. She won several awards, including first place in a *Bell's Letters* contest. Following that, her varied career branched into book reviews for several periodicals, including *The Bloomsbury Review.*

Goldberg's researching skills have played a major role in her endeavors. She has written extensively in the occupations area for *Career World Magazine, American Careers,* and the many career publications offered by CASS Recruitment Corporation and The Dartnell Corporation. She has also contributed to a number of projects for educational publishers including Scott Foresman, Addison Wesley, and Britannica Learning Centers including textbooks for reading and science and the creation of a literature-based reading/writing program. Recently, she completed rewriting and revising an educational activity book for Camp Fire Boys and Girls.

As a magazine writer, Goldberg's 200-plus articles have appeared in *Opportunity Magazine, Complete Woman, North Shore Magazine, Today's Chicago Woman, Chicago Parent,* and the Pioneer Press newspapers. In addition she has authored three books for VGM: *Careers in Journalism* (1995), *Opportunities in Horticulture Careers* (1995), and *On the Job: Real People Working in Communications* (1996).

ACKNOWLEDGMENTS

The author gratefully acknowledges the professionals who graciously agreed to be profiled within and all of the associations and organizations that provided valuable and interesting information.

Special thanks to Deborah L. Sattley, Ph.D. candidate at the Jane Addams College of Social Work, Chicago, Illinois, for her cooperation, plentiful supply of useful information, and authoring of the Foreword for this book.

My dear husband, Larry; daughters, Sherri and Debbie; sister, Adrienne; and brother, Paul, for their encouragement and support.

Family and close friends Mindi, Cary, Michele, Bruce, Michele, Alison, Steven, Marty, Marci, Steven, Brian, Jesse, and Bertha.

A special thanks to a special friend, Diana Catlin.

Sincere gratitude to Betsy Lancefield, Associate Editor/VGM Career Books, for providing this challenging opportunity and a disposition that makes all projects rewarding and enjoyable.

FOREWORD

Research and development are at the very heart of all of the scientific venues: the biological and medical sciences; the argricultural sciences; the physical sciences; computer and mathematical sciences; and the social sciences. Throughout history, all advancements that have been made are a direct result of the efforts of people with inquisitive minds who have a love and respect for their fellow man. Their search to uncover new truths affects every aspect of our lives.

In the area of the social sciences, survey and marketing research are the primary sources of up-to-date information needed by government for everything from the state of the nation's health and family incomes to the public's preference in consumer products and political attitudes. Economic indicators like the Gross National Product (GNP), unemployment rate, and cost-of-living index are all used by government agencies in operating major social programs like Social Security and unemployment compensation. Information about social indicators such as mortality rate and marriage and divorce figures enable Congress, agencies, and business to anticipate the future needs of society.

The statistics from standardized (and other types of) testing allow educators to measure progress, schools to select the candidates with the most merit, and employers to choose the most promising employees.

Social science research enables us to understand how and why we interact as we do. It allows us to gather data about human behavior, look for patterns, construct hypotheses to account for the trends, and proceed with methods to test possible explanations and provide alternative solutions to societal concerns.

In short, social science research is a tool that allows us to trace human development over the span of years, decades, even centuries. To be sure, being a part of this is a wonderfully worthwhile endeavor.

Deborah L. Sattley
Research Assistant
Jane Addams College of Social Work
Chicago, Illinois

PREFACE

A column in a recent Juvenile Diabetes Foundation International newsletter explains the process, the importance, and the urgency of research. It features a letter from its president, Willard J. Overlock, Jr.:

> In the movie *Field of Dreams,* the main character had a vision and worked tirelessly to achieve it, despite the doubts of others. He believed that if he created what was necessary for an event to happen, it would. "If you build it, they will come . . ." This is the passion of the Juvenile Diabetes Foundation. From the first half dozen research grants funded twenty-five years ago, we are now funding hundreds of researchers each year all over the world, all aimed at curing diabetes and its complications.
>
> JDF is a twenty-six-year-old voluntary, nonprofit organization with 110 chapters in the United States and ten affiliates worldwide. Funds are raised through a variety of special events, direct mail memberships, "Walks for the cure," and The Only Remedy Is a Cure campaign. In our history, JDF has given more than $180 million to diabetes research—more than any other nongovernmental health agency in the world.
>
> We utilize a two-tier peer-review process. First a scientific committee evaluates grant submissions based on excellence in science. Then a lay review committee evaluates how well this excellent science relates to the goals of JDF. We fund grants that range from early training for young scientists to sophisticated multicenter, multidisciplinary approaches to a cure. The subject matter of these grants covers every possible detail relating to the eradication of this disease.
>
> We continue to build and "they" continue to come; people who raise funds for research—the dollars needed to fund more and better projects—and those who do the research. When JDF's vision is achieved, we will be known as the people who cured diabetes.

DEDICATION

To my husband, Larry, for his continual love and support.
To my daughters, Sherri and Debbie, for always believing in me.
And to the memory of my father and mother, Sam and Sylvia Lefkovitz, for encouraging me to follow my dreams.

CHAPTER 1

OVERVIEW OF RESEARCH
AND DEVELOPMENT

Basic research is what I'm doing when I don't know what I'm doing.

—Werner von Braun

Are you the kind of person who looks for answers to things? Do you enjoy uncovering information? Do you have an affinity for Sherlock Holmes? Are you good at discovering things? Then perhaps you would do well to pursue the idea of working as a researcher in any number of fields. Researchers work in virtually every industry in addition to government, not-for-profit segments, and every other arena you can think of. And the payoffs are great. Because of research, we have preventative shots for measles and mumps, more advanced computer equipment virtually every day, better tasting and more nutritional "TV" dinners, and more efficient medications.

Do any of the following want ads sound appealing to you? These are the kinds of people the world of research is seeking. Try to picture yourself as one of them:

Research Opportunities
Our large, not-for-profit organization has an immediate need for research associates. We seek degreed candidates with backgrounds in the behavioral or social sciences and working knowledge of statistics and database management. In exchange for your expertise, we offer a

salary in the upper 30s/low 40s, an excellent work environment, and a convenient location. To apply, send resume.

Postdoctoral Research Fellow
F/T position available immediately at large medical center located in suburbs, 10 miles west of downtown busy city. Successful candidate will be involved in investigative studies concerning the molecular mechanisms of cell aging, specifically addressing the roles of repressor oncogenes in modulating mitogenic and chemotactic behavior cells. Cell and molecular biology experience required, D.D.S., Ph.D., or M.D. with appropriate postdoctoral training preferred, although not necessary. Salary commensurate with qualifications and experience. Interested candidates, please send curriculum vitae and three reference letters.

Research Chemist
XXXX Company, a specialty chemical manufacturer, and a division of YYY Corp., has a career opportunity at our local site. The ideal candidate will possess an M.S. in chemistry with 5–10 years experience in the development of structural adhesives, sealants, and underbody coatings. Supervisory experience and superior interpersonal skills required. We offer a salary commensurate with experience and an attractive benefits package. Please send your resume with salary requirements in confidence.

Clinical Research Associate
Regional position for international contract research organization. Degree in science or health preferred. Previous research experience required, 2 years monitoring preferred. Conduct all aspects of pharmaceutical research. Extensive travel required. If you are flexible, autonomous, and self-directed, send resume and salary requirements.

Research Technologist
Autonomic Pharmacology Lab
Must have experience in basic pharmacology techniques including isotope technology, small animal organ and tissue level pharmacology, and

a familiarity with protein chemistry. Computer experience in Microsoft Word and Excel helpful. Send resume.

R & D—Bakery

Multistate gourmet fresh-frozen bakery manufacturing company seeks growth necessitated R & D position. Responsible for ongoing development. Must have a love of baking! Food science or related degree required. Frozen baked goods experience preferred. Send resume with salary requirements.

Research and development is a vast field that exists within a multitude of other fields. Since it would be impossible to delve into every area of research and development, the author has chosen a number of notables as representative of the possibilities in this field. It is by no means all inclusive. Virtually every existing field or area has a segment or subsection of research and development within it. For those of you who enjoy looking for answers, explanations, improvements, and new ways to do things; like making discoveries and testing new ideas; and find the idea of advancing civilization and humanity appealing; research is the perfect choice!

CHAPTER 2

THE BIOLOGICAL AND MEDICAL SCIENCES

Not many appreciate the ultimate power and potential usefulness of basic knowledge accumulated by obscure, unseen investigators who, in a lifetime of intensive study, may never see any practical use for their findings but who go on seeking answers to the unknown without thought of financial or practical gain.

—Eugenie Clark (United States Marines biologist, author)

Does the thought of delving into the study of living organisms and their environmental relationships sound appealing to you? Then consider venturing into a career as a biological or medical scientist!

Large numbers of biological and medical scientists work in research and development taking on any one of many specialties ranging from botany (the study of plants) to microbiology (the study of microscopic organisms) to zoology (the study of animals).

Working in the areas of either basic or applied research, biological and medical scientists attempt to increase our knowledge of living organisms. Those who focus on applied research take the knowledge gained in basic research and apply it to a variety of diverse and important areas, such as creating new medicines, upgrading our environment, and increasing crop yields.

BIOTECHNOLOGY

In recent years there has been a dramatic thrust in the area of biotechnology, spurred by advances in basic biological know how, particularly in the area of genetics. As a result of these advances, biological and medical scientists (particularly biochemists and molecular biologists) are able to manipulate the genetic material of plants and animals in order to improve on what already exists; for instance, making organisms more resistant to disease.

The term *biotechnology* refers to processes like gene splicing, cell fusion, and other methods of controlling the genetic material of living things. Initial applications to this technology have been in the medical and pharmaceutical areas, where a number of substances that were not previously available in substantial quantities are beginning to be produced through biotechnological means. It already has led to mass production of scarce biochemicals, such as growth hormones and human insulin, and opened up possibilities for commercial applications in agriculture.

BIOLOGICAL AND MEDICAL SPECIALTIES

A vast number of specialties are open to biologists (with considerable overlapping of areas or concentrations). They include:

Microbiologists

These scientists study the characteristics and growth of organisms that are microscopic, for example, algae, protozoa, or bacteria. Research microbiologists concentrate on the biological, biochemical, and physical qualities of microorganisms that cause disease in an attempt to discover how they both cause and transmit diseases.

Part of a microbiologist's work is to perform physical, serological, or chemical tests on vast numbers of specific microorganisms. In order to accomplish this, electron microscopes, DNA analyzers, optical microscopes, amino acids, and other equipment are utilized. Other typical procedures include injecting infected body fluids into laboratory animals and observing them closely for the symptoms of disease, extracting blood from laboratory animals, or performing postmortem examinations to discover the toxic effects of the disease-carrying microorganisms.

To keep us safe from food poisoning, microbiologists study foodborne diseases and toxin-producing bacteria in an attempt to find new ways to prevent contamination of food. To their credit, they have already developed vaccines, toxoids, and antiserums that prevent yellow fever, polio, measles, smallpox, and influenza. And, as of this writing, they are hard at work finding cures for cancer, diabetes, cystic fibrosis, AIDS, and Alzheimer's disease.

Microbiologists make use of their experimentation skills and knowledge in various fields and are employed in industries such as textiles, agriculture, cosmetics, paper, industrial chemicals, and pharmaceuticals.

Subcategories of microbiologists include the following:

Clinical microbiologists. These scientists isolate and identify microorganisms from animals and humans with clinical diseases. Once subjecting disease-causing bacteria cultures to antimicrobial agents, microbiologists focus on discovering an antibiotic that will control that bacteria.

Virologists. These scientists focus specifically on viruses. After injecting viral matter into animals, eggs, or tissue cultures, they observe any changes caused by the viruses. They search for answers to how viruses infect and reproduce in cells and how they cause disease.

Mycologists. These scientists study the life processes of poisonous, edible, and parasitic fungi in an attempt to find which are of use in agriculture, industry, or medicine. After study, they apply their findings to the development of drugs and medicines. Some mycologists specialize in a particular field, such as antibiotics.

Immunologists. These scientists study the ability of the body to resist disease. To this end, they measure antibodies against bacterial and viral disease-causing organisms, examine immunoglobulins in patients, perform blood grouping, and investigate transplant rejections by the body's immune system.

Biochemists. These scientists focus on the chemical components of living things in an attempt to understand the complex chemical combinations and reactions that are part of the processes of growth, heredity, reproduction, and metabolism.

As the name suggests, biochemistry is both a biological science and a branch of chemistry. The science seeks to find answers to questions like the following: How does food intake govern life processes? How does the genetic information inside these organisms control the processes going on?

Up until recently, biochemists focused on causes and effects, but now they are starting to focus more on how to control the things that happen. An important possibility of biochemical genetic research is the potential to find out how to predict and treat genetic diseases by understanding how genes operate.

A typical day for biochemists and/or their assistants includes weighing, filtering, distilling, and drying substances; creating microorganism and viral cultures; cultivating plants secured to controlled areas; and taking care of laboratory animals. In addition they utilize complicated instruments like the spectrometer, a device used to measure molecular magnetic properties. The measurement of reactions of cells, tissues, and body fluids may call for these researchers to design and construct equipment.

Biochemists need to be comfortable working with mathematical and chemical equations and computers because their work dictates proficiency in these areas. Compiling their findings, they write reports that may later become published documents.

Biochemists may deal with the following issues: obesity, viral infection, aging, alcoholism, and the causes of disease. Their concerns even include examining the biochemical and physiological changes that astronauts undergo as a result of being in space.

Some biochemists work in agriculture on projects such as crop cultivation, animal nutrition, or genetic engineering. Those involved in nutrition are assigned duties of analyzing food products to measure vitamins, carbohydrates, minerals, proteins, and other compounds within them.

Biochemists known as clinical chemists work in pharmaceutical or medical laboratories conducting or directing tests performed on body fluids such as blood or urine. These tests are used to confirm a physician's diagnosis, to screen for evidence of disease, and to gauge a patient's recovery. In the pharmaceutical industry, clinical chemists design, develop, and evaluate drugs, antibiotics, and other medical aids.

Biochemists who are employed by hospitals may need to be certified by a board that engages in national certification, such as the American Board of Clinical Chemistry.

Pharmacologists

These scientists explore drug action, both therapeutic and toxic, on biological systems. It is a science that is fundamental not only to medicine but also to pharmacy, nursing, dentistry, and veterinary medicine. The word *pharmacology* comes from the Greek *pharmakon,* meaning a drug or medicine, and *logos,* meaning the truth about or a rational discussion.

Building upon the knowledge obtained in other sciences such as physics, chemistry, mathematics, and engineering, pharmacologists often work together to develop complex drugs and drug compounds effective in treating a variety of diseases. The use of insulin for diabetics, antibiotics such as penicillin, tranquilizers, and the polio vaccine are just a few discoveries attributable to pharmacologists. And the boundaries continue to expand. Recently, pharmacologists have been concerned with the production of medicines in space as well as the effects of drugs on people in space.

Pharmacologists ask questions like: What changes in the brain are responsible for depression? What agents will be most effective in treating these conditions?

Pharmacologists may be employed by academic institutions, private research firms, and government institutions in research centers such as the Environmental Protection Agency (EPA) and the Food and Drug Administration (FDA).

In general there are two paths leading to a career in pharmacology. Students enrolled in medical schools may specialize in pharmacology during medical studies or following the attainment of an M.D. degree. Another possibility is through a course of study in a graduate school leading to a Ph.D. in pharmacology. Since pharmacology is not offered in most undergraduate programs, students usually major in chemistry, one of the biological sciences, or in pharmacy, although a student's undergraduate degree doesn't have to be in science in order for him or her to be accepted to a graduate school that offers a Ph.D. in pharmacology. However, coursework in physics, organic and physical chemistry, along with math and statistics is helpful.

The American Society for Pharmacology and Experimental Therapeutics offers a summer fellowship program for undergraduates in this field. Ph.D. programs are offered in medical schools, pharmacy schools, schools of veterinary medicine, and graduate schools of biomedical sciences. As is the case in other scientific fields, postdoctoral research is done routinely.

THE PHARMACEUTICAL INDUSTRY

Pharmacologists should not be confused with pharmacists. While pharmacologists are researchers who work with the basic and clinical sciences dealing with the interactions between chemicals and biological systems, pharmacists are health professionals who follow the prescriptions of physicians to prepare and dispense drugs and medicines to patients.

Pharmacists with bachelor's degrees may work as laboratory scientists, clinical assistants, or drug registration specialists. Those with advanced degrees usually work in pharmaceutics, industrial pharmacy, pharmaceutical chemistry, or biopharmaceutics. Some employed by pharmaceutical companies may direct work in research and product development. They may supervise research and laboratory assistants working on assigned projects, and they may collect data and write up technical reports.

Today approximately twelve percent of all pharmacists in industry are in research and development. Major pharmaceutical companies spend literally billions of dollars each year for research and development. About ten percent of pharmaceutical research is basic research. Eighty-five percent is devoted to applied research projects, while product improvement accounts for the remainder.

Most pharmaceutical research is initiated when a drug needs to be tested for safety in animals and future clinical studies for humans. Tests begin with the chemistry, stability, and compatibility of the drug substance, and formulation starts to plan how the drug will be dispensed—perhaps tablets or liquid.

As an example, Ehrlich and Landsteiner discovered the antigen-antibody reaction, the process that protects the body from foreign or toxic substances. Further research on suppressing this immune response facilitated the development of successful organ transplants.

The applications of pharmacology to health and agriculture have resulted in the widespread growth of the drug manufacturing industry. Large numbers of pharmacologists are hired by national pharmaceutical corporations to develop new products or to improve those already existing. Work is usually done as part of large multidisciplinary groups that include chemists, biochemists, and toxicologists.

Toxicologists. These scientists perform research designed to determine the possible adverse or toxic effects of drugs and other chemical agents on plants, animals, and human beings. Often considered a subcategory of pharmacology, toxicologists usually work closely together with pharmacologists and other scientific researchers.

Given the opportunity, toxicologists might have been able to change the course of history because they would have known hundreds of years ago that the lead pipes that carried drinking water and the lead bowls that contained wines and syrups could leak lead into food and drink. Since only the rich were able to afford piped water and wines and syrups, lead poisoning was responsible for a drop in the number of healthy children born to the wealthy. Over the course of many centuries, this loss could well have been a contributing factor to the fall of the Roman Empire.

Toxicologists working in research are employed by industries, government, research institutions, and universities. In many cases projects are long-term studies designed to enhance our basic understanding of life processes and of the mechanisms by which toxic materials produce their effects.

Pharmaceutical businesses employ large numbers of toxicologists to test new drugs to determine if they are safe for human beings and to find out how the drugs work. As a result, many potentially harmful drugs never reach store shelves.

Together, pharmacologists and toxicologists study toxic materials such as lead or mercury in the workplace. In addition, they examine household items such as aerosol sprays to determine what effects, if any, they have on humans and our environment. Additionally, they may seek to find chemicals that will harm only certain pests.

Amadeo J. Pesce, Ph.D.

Dr. Pesce serves as Professor of Pathology, Director of the Toxicology Laboratory, Professor of Experimental Medicine at the University of

Cincinnati Hospital. He has been associated with the University of Cincinnati for the past twenty-three years.

"I always knew I was interested in medical research," says Dr. Pesce. "So that's where I was focused early on. I earned my undergraduate degree at the Massachusetts Institute of Technology. Then I attended Brandeis University for my graduate degree in biochemistry. My postdoctoral scholarship was at the University of Illinois at Champaign-Urbana.

"To do this kind of work you need to have Ph.D. credentials. I also have board certification by the American Board for Clinical Chemistry, which I think is very important. (Certification is given to those who have the proper scientific background, five years experience in the field, and successful completion of an examination.)

"In most cases I work as part of a team of researchers. The composition of the team may change depending on the project. Participants may include postdoctoral fellows, part-time or full-time technologists, pathologists, mathematicians, psychiatrists, substance abuse counselors, and other health and scientific professionals.

"Usually there are several projects going on at the same time. For instance, we're now helping with the clinical trials in developing methods of measurement for a couple of different projects. One project is to help pace patients by monitoring the effectiveness of the drug called AZT, which is used in the treatment of AIDS. We've developed the technology to measure the concentration of drugs inside the cell and are working very closely with the clinician and the clinical trials that are being conducted.

"Another project we're participating in is the study of developing agents that will help combat substance abuse by reducing the craving and the other aspects that make people want to continue to use drugs. In this project, we work with a group of psychiatrists and substance abuse counselors, and they provide specimens from the patients for us to monitor.

"In addition to the hours spent in the laboratory, a considerable portion of my time is spent thinking and writing. One must think things through and be able to communicate them effectively and efficiently in order for the research to have meaning. And as I teach my students—If it's not written down, it was never done.

"As an administrator, I have other responsibilities: I supervise a postdoctoral fellow and I handle personnel issues and administrative problems. And at this point in my life, I accomplish this and keep fairly regular working hours. But when I was younger (and for many years), I worked from seven in the morning until ten at night, five days a week. The other two days I *only* worked eight to ten hours a day. This was not required, but just my own enthusiasm showing, based upon my decision to be one of the four most recognized people in the field. So I set on a path of learning all I could and then proceeded to put out a series of books, (eighteen), about the field. This required an immense amount of work. I tell everyone I did this to become rich and famous (my children always told me to skip the fame!). But as it turns out, all I got was the fame. However, even though I didn't make the money I had hoped for, it has still been very rewarding. Fans as far away as Australia have asked me to sign their copy of one of my books.

"This career has many other rewards; uppermost is the accomplishment of developing a theory and finding supporting data. (After all, projects are funded grants for which you must show results by a certain date in order to be funded for the next project.) On the down side, the worst part of the job is when you write a paper and its gets rejected by your peers (and you think they're wrong, and in fact you know they're wrong). The real issue for me is that we've done some pioneering work for people that has been fruitful and rewarding.

"Here's an example. A while back we developed a way of looking at cancer in mice, and a colleague working on cancer research sent me a letter commending me on the work. The fact that somebody would think enough of our work to take what we've done and build on it is very rewarding.

"Another accomplishment relates to transplant patients. Some of the drugs used to treat these patients are very expensive, and we were able to devise a way of cutting the cost of those drugs from about $6,000 a year to about $1,200. This means that Third World countries can actually afford the drug for their transplant patients. That's quite an accomplishment.

"To be doing this kind of work, it helps to have an understanding partner as I did. And since it is so important to be able to interact with people, exchange ideas, and get them to help with particular areas of your project, you must have the ability to get along with all kinds of people. You have to be aware of what issues others have and be able to accommodate them so they'll accommodate you in return. I have found that this is the proper approach to a successful collaboration. It's not unlike working with others on a book or any other project in which a number of people need to extend themselves in order to fulfill a common goal."

OTHER SUBSPECIALTIES

Medical microbiologists. These researchers focus on the relationship between organisms and disease or the effects of antibiotics on microorganisms. Some microbiologists specialize in food, agriculture, industry, or the environment.

Aquatic biologists. These scientists concentrate on plants and animal species who are exclusive to water.

Marine biologists. These scientists focus only on saltwater organisms. Marine biologists are sometimes called oceanographers, but since oceanographers study the physical characteristics of oceans and the ocean floor, they would more correctly be grouped with geologists and geophysicists (see Chapter 4).

Limnologists. The "flipside" of marine biologists, limnologists study only organisms found in freshwater.

Botanists. These well-known scientists study plants and their surrounding environment. They may incorporate all aspects of plant life or specialize in a particular area, for example, causes and cures of plant diseases.

Pathologists. These researchers study the effects of parasites, diseases, and insects on human cells, tissues, and organs.

Physiologists. Physiologists focus on life processes in both plants and animals. They may specialize in areas such as respiration, reproduction, or photosynthesis.

Environmentalists. These researchers seek answers to environmental problems like hazardous waste, chemical dumping, and the environmental consequences of industry.

This broad scientific category includes disciplines such as hazardous and solid-waste management, chemical engineering, air and water quality, geology, geophysics, conservation, meteorology, ecology, economics, geology, botany, biology, sociology, zoology, and anthropology.

A new job category, this field encompasses many other scientific disciplines. Anticipated growth is based upon government, corporate, and public concern about the effects of hazardous waste, global warming, oil spills and fires, acid rain, deterioration of the ozone layer, toxic emissions, wildlife extinction, destruction of tropical rain forests, and other environmental problems caused by humans.

An emerging consumer field will be environmental diagnostics, which involves the development of kits ordinary citizens can use to test food, water, or other substances for pesticide residues, food contaminants, and industrial pollutants. This new technique, called "immunoassays," analyzes and measures the concentration of chemicals.

Likely employers include the Environmental Protection Agency and the Occupational Safety and Health Administration.

Zoologists. Perhaps easiest to identify, zoologists study animals; everything from their origin to their behavior to all body processes and functions. They may do experiments with live animals or dissections of dead animals in their effort to uncover information. Zoologists are often given more specific names based upon a further specialty, such as ornithologists (birds) or ichthyologists (fish).

Ecologists. These scientists focus on relationships; those between organisms and their environment and additional influences such as temperature or altitude.

Medical scientists. This is the name given to scientists who perform biomedical research. When working on basic research, medical scientists usually strive to determine the causes and treatments for diseases and other health problems. For instance, they may attempt to locate the types of changes apparent in a cell, chromosome, or gene that indicates the beginnings of a health problem such as cancer. Once an identification has been made, medical scientists work toward some kind of treatment. For example, a medical scientist working in cancer research might devise a treatment for cancer in the form of a combination of drugs that results in the lessening of the disease's effects.

If the medical scientist has an actual degree in medicine, he or she could administer a drug to patients on a clinical trial basis, then monitor its effects and document the findings. Those who do not have medical degrees themselves work in conjunction with those who do. Bringing the results back to the laboratory, the medical scientist can then examine the results and decide whether dosages need to be adjusted.

Besides using basic research techniques to create treatments for existing health problems, medical scientists also work toward inhibiting or preventing health problems, such as confirming the link between alcoholism and liver disease.

EDUCATION AND TRAINING

At the high school level, those interested in the biological sciences should concentrate on a college entrance curriculum consisting of biology, chemistry, physics, algebra, geometry, trigonometry, computer science, mathematics, English, and a foreign language. Participation in science fairs, science clubs, and National Science Foundation programs are considered a real plus.

A substantial number of colleges and universities offer undergraduate degrees in biological science. However, all set up their own degree requirements, so if you plan to pursue a master's or doctorate, make sure that the undergraduate college or university you attend fulfills any required courses and credits you may need. Undergraduate majors can vary—microbiology, chemistry, biochemistry, or a related degree are all okay. Just be sure to concentrate on building a solid foundation in the biological and physical sciences. Focus on biology, biochemistry, mathematics, computer science, statistics, and physics. Other worthwhile classes include organic and inorganic chemistry, calculus, and other specialty courses such as genetics, physiology, zoology, or microbiology. Standard classes such as English, economics, sociology, and history should also be included. Some schools offer both bachelor of science (B.S.) and bachelor of arts (B.A.) degrees.

The National Science Foundation and the National Institutes of Health sponsor research programs at the undergraduate level. Some universities offer training programs for specialized laboratory techniques that other researchers and companies find important. These "certificate programs" may transfer such skills as genetic engineering, recombinant DNA technology, cell culture, biotechnology, in vitro cell biology, or protein engineering. Sometimes you can work toward both a bachelor's degree and a certificate at the same time.

Requirements for a master's degree include about two years of concentrated studies including course work, fieldwork, and an original research project culminating in a formally written thesis.

Completion of a Ph.D. requires course work, original research, and a formally written thesis. This usually takes approximately four years. The research project is vital because it is designed to enable the Ph.D. candidate to develop the ability to isolate scientific questions and discover ways to get answers, as well as to teach the laboratory skills required to tackle a vast number of biochemical problems.

According to a survey from the Council of Graduate Schools in Washington DC, biologists have an unusually deep quest for graduate level study. Although 23 percent of all undergraduates (as a whole) make the choice to go on to graduate school, an amazing 81 percent of biological science majors continue on to that level. No other field even comes close to this.

Even those who have earned a Ph.D. usually continue their learning through two or three years of postdoctoral research. Since these fields are ever changing with frequent breakthroughs in technology, scientists often seek out such assignments before they take permanent jobs. Usually there is no formal course work, no degree credit, and no teaching involved. But these research assignments are sought because individuals then have a chance to work on a full-time high-level research project in the laboratory of a scientist who is already established. Researchers often receive a salary or fellowship.

Because medical scientists work almost entirely in research, the absolute minimum required for a prospective medical scientist is a Ph.D. With this credential you can perform research on basic life processes or specific medical diseases or problems. From this research you are able to analyze and interpret the results of experiments on patients. Those who administer drug or gene therapy to humans or who in some other way interact on a medical basis with patients (drawing blood for example) must have a medical degree.

Besides formal education requirements, medical scientists are expected to successfully complete several years in a postdoctoral position. This work provides valuable laboratory experience and sometimes provides an entry into a salaried full-time position.

Biological and medical scientists must be able to perform well on an independent basis or as a member of a team. Communication skills are of the utmost importance in order to impart the information gleaned both orally and in writing.

Above average intelligence, capacity for hard work, curiosity, logical thinking, and initiative are also considered desirable qualities. Others include the ability to abandon unworkable theories, withstand the ensuing disappointment, and begin a project anew.

WORKING ENVIRONMENT

Biological and medical scientists sometimes work fairly regular hours in laboratories and offices. However, work may need to be taken home, literature may need to be read during off hours, or additional time may need to be put in at the workplace. This will vary according to your specific position, where you are working, and the project you are presently working on.

Biological and medical scientists working in research are typically found in laboratories making use of computers, thermal cyclers, electron microscopes, and many other pieces of scientific equipment. However, depending on the project, considerable work may be accomplished outside the laboratory, such as in the case of a botanist studying the plant species that thrive in tropical rain forests or other biological or medical scientists who conduct experiments on laboratory animals or greenhouse plants.

In some cases dangerous organisms or toxic substances may be involved in laboratory experimentation, and strict safety procedures must be followed carefully to avoid contamination.

EMPLOYMENT

A recent survey reports that biological and medical scientists number approximately 120,000. This is not counting the professionals who hold faculty positions at colleges or universities.

About 70 percent of biochemists work in pure research. Most of the remaining numbers are involved in applied research where new products are developed based upon what was learned through basic research. Some biochemists with Ph.D.'s choose to perform administrative work with well-known institutions such as the National Science Foundation or the National Institutes of Health. Others may become top individuals in hospital clinic laboratories, university departments, or research laboratories.

About 40 percent of nonfaculty biological scientists are employed by federal, state, and local governments. In the federal government, this includes the U.S. Departments of the Interior, Agriculture, and Defense. Most of the rest work in hospitals, research and testing laboratories, or in the pharmaceutical industry. Of medical scientists, 20 percent work in research and testing laboratories, while the rest work in the pharmaceutical industry or hospitals.

Some biological and medical scientists are managers or administrators planning and/or overseeing programs; for example, one involving the testing of drugs, foods, or other products.

Job Prospects

According to the United States Department of Labor's *Occupational Outlook Handbook,* employment of biological and medical scientists is expected to increase faster than the average for all occupations through the year 2005. This is because biological and medical scientists will be needed to continue to conduct biotechnological and genetic research and aid in the development of new products produced by innovative biological methods. Health issues such as AIDS, cancer, and the human genome project should also result in growing numbers. However, some belt tightening in federal government budgets could result in slower employment growth in the public sector and even in some private industries that rely on government grants.

Another area of growth is the popular campaign to clean up and preserve our environment. Biological and other scientists and engineers will be called upon to find ways to correct past (and present) environmental transgressions.

Due to increasing specialization in science, the demand for toxicologists is high with an advantage over some other scientists like biologists or chemists. Positions with the federal government will be particularly possible in such agencies as the Centers for Disease Control in Atlanta (CDC), the Environmental Protection Agency (EPA), or the Food and Drug Administration (FDA).

PROFESSIONAL ASSOCIATIONS

A large number of professional associations are available to those in this field. They provide networking opportunities and a professional support system for individuals who have similar concerns and interests. A sampling of possibilities are named below.

The American Society for Microbiology is a popular group numbering about 38,000 in membership. Through reports, discussions, and publications, the organization promotes scientific knowledge of the field. A smaller association, the Society for Industrial Microbiology has about 1,850 members. Another group, The American Institute of Biological Sciences, is a federation of research societies and laboratories that focuses on the life sciences. It's membership consists of approximately 7,200 individuals.

Other organizations include the American Society for Biochemistry and Molecular Biology and the American Association for Clinical Chemistry.

The American Chemical Society (ACS) offers a *Directory of Graduate Research* that provides information about graduate programs in biochemistry. For pharmacologists the major organization is the American Society for Pharmacology and Experimental Therapeutics (ASPET).

Others include the American Society for Clinical Pharmacology and Therapeutics, the American Association of Pharmaceutical Scientists, and the American College of Neuropsychopharmacology.

For toxicologists there is the Society of Toxicology, the American Board of Medical Toxicology, and the American Academy of Clinical Toxicology.

SALARIES

Earnings fluctuate depending on the area of the country, specialty, your education and experience, size of the company, and nature of the job assignment. Generally private industry pays better than education, government, or health care. Usually based upon a forty-hour week, a recent survey found that a median annual salary for biological and life scientists is about $35,000. For medical scientists, median annual salaries are about $33,000. According to the College Placement Council, starting salary offers in private industry averaged approximately $22,000 for those with a bachelor's degree in biological science. Those with a master's degree may expect about $30,000 per year, and those with doctoral degrees can expect an average of $34,500 per year.

A recent survey issued by the College Placement Council reports that individuals with bachelor's degrees in chemistry can expect about $29,000; those with doctoral degrees in chemistry can expect beginning salaries of approximately $50,000 a year. Biochemists with experience who work for the federal government may reach a GS-15 rating, which now pays approximately $65,000.

Federal government statistics list general biological scientists in non-supervisory, supervisory, and managerial positions at about $46,000, microbiologists at about $50,000, ecologists at about $45,000, physiologists at about $56,000, and geneticists at about $56,000.

Salaries for pharmacologists are among the highest in the world of scientific occupations. Though figures always vary according to specialty, experience, skills, and position, recent surveys show that beginning pharmacologists with a doctorate earned more than $50,000 a year. Those with supervisory responsibilities may earn more than $100,000 a year.

Toxicologists with master's degrees can expect to receive approximately $25,000 to $32,000 to start. Those with doctoral degrees and a few years of experience may earn from $55,000 all the way up to $90,000 per year. Executive toxicology positions may pay more than $100,000.

FOR ADDITIONAL INFORMATION

Additional information is available from the following sources:

American Board of Toxicology, Inc.
1101 Fourteenth Street, NW, Suite 1100
Washington, DC 20005

American Council on Pharmaceutical Education
311 West Superior Street
Chicago, IL 60610

American Pharmaceutical Association
2215 Constitution Avenue, NW
Washington, DC 20037–2985

American Physiological Society
Membership Services Department
9650 Rockville Pike
Bethesda, MD 20814

American Society for Biochemistry and Molecular Biology
9650 Rockville Pike
Bethesda, MD 20814

American Society for Microbiology
Office of Education and Training—Career Information
1325 Massachusetts Avenue NW
Washington, DC 20005

American Society for Pharmacology and Experimental Therapeutics, Inc.
9650 Rockville Pike
Bethesda, MD 20814

American Society of Zoologists
P.O. Box 2739
California Lutheran University
Thousand Oaks, CA 91360

Environmental Opportunities
Box 788
Walpole, NH 03608

National Association of Environmental Professionals
P.O. Box 9400
Washington, DC 20016

Society for Industrial Microbiology
P.O. Box 329
Annandale, VA 22003-8329

Society of Toxicology
1101 Fourteenth Street, NW, Suite 1100
Washington, DC 20005

CHAPTER 3

THE AGRICULTURAL SCIENCES

The way to do research is to attack the facts at the point of greatest astonishment.

—Celia Green, *The Decline and Fall of Science* (1977)

Ever wonder where frozen dinners came from? Or dry packaged soups? Or frozen concentrated orange juice? Or freeze-dried coffee?

They are the direct result of the efforts of men and women in food technology who apply scientific knowledge to product research and development. Sensitive to demands for greater varieties of nutritious foods in convenient forms, it is the food scientist who applies the advances in basic research, process engineering, and packaging innovations to satisfy the consumer—you and me.

Food scientists are part of a general category known as agricultural scientists.

AGRICULTURAL SCIENTISTS

Agricultural scientists study animals and farm crops in an attempt to develop new avenues of improving both quality and quantity. They endeavor to increase crop yields, while at the same time minimize labor, control pests, and conserve supplies of water and soil.

Agricultural science may be considered closely related to, or part of, the biological sciences. Agricultural scientists make use of biology, chemistry, and additional sciences to isolate problems and formulate solutions in the world of agriculture. Often they team up with biological scientists working on biological research and are able to apply what is learned in the field of biotechnology to agriculture.

Four large subcategories of agricultural science are featured below:

FOOD SCIENCE

Food science is an important career of the future because it combines sophisticated technology with the widespread concern for proper nutrition and fitness.

Usually hired by the food processing industry, food scientists or technologists strive to satisfy the consumer's continual desire for new edibles and new ways of preparing or processing foods. The public demands a wide variety of product choices and wants them to be convenient, low in calories, high in nutrition, tasty, microwaveable, low in fat, safe, healthy, and enjoyable or effective. This is accomplished through improved methods of preserving, processing, packaging, storing, and delivering goods brought about by the effective use of microbiology, chemistry, and a sampling of other sciences. New and better food sources are also important to developing countries and those suffering from famine.

Some food scientists are involved in basic research looking for new sources of food and substitutes for harmful additives or analyzing the content of food to ascertain existing quantities of fat, sugar, protein, or vitamins. A day's work might consist of testing the color, flavor, texture, and nutritive value of food or testing samples for yeasts, molds, and bacteria that may make products harmful or lessen their "shelf" life.

While some food technologists are employed by product development operations, others are responsible for inspecting food processing areas and enforcing government regulations. Food scientists may also be employed by universities and the federal government.

Food scientists in private industry may find themselves in test kitchens investigating techniques for processing a new food. Staffed with professional chefs or economists, food scientists work hand-in-hand to create the best possible product. To this end food scientists may work with microbiologists, sensory evaluation experts, engineers, statisticians, packaging specialists, and marketing experts.

After a new product is developed, food scientists work on setting up the necessary steps to produce the food at a reasonable cost, setting proper safety and quality standards.

Food scientists may specialize in one specific food group such as grains, dairy products, fats and oils, or fish and seafoods. One such subspecialty is cereal science.

Cereal Science

Cereal scientists study the chemical composition and physical structure of cereals and their relationship to grain quality (nutritional quality, processing quality, and product quality). Cereal researchers work with agronomists and cereal breeders to develop new cereal varieties with better quality, disease resistance, and higher yields. Because of the world's rapidly expanding population, research on improved crop varieties is very important to ensure an adequate food supply.

Cereal chemists who work in product development use their ingenuity to develop new processes or products. This would include formulating new products from existing ingredients, improving the flavor of a product, conducting tests, measuring nutrients, or finding new uses for underutilized cereals and their by-products. Working in product development also requires a knowledge of the properties of cereals and how these properties are affected by combining cereals with other ingredients or perhaps using different processing methods.

Both curiosity and creativity are important qualities of a cereal chemist. While in training they must learn sophisticated analytical procedures that must be used to study the biochemical components of cereals.

Educational requirements vary depending on the specific job area and level of responsibility. Many types of institutions offer appropriate programs from two-year technical degrees to four-year bachelor of science degrees to graduate degrees (master's or doctorates). Most of the individuals engaged in cereal research have postgraduate degrees.

If you were a cereal scientist about to begin a job with General Mills, Inc., at the James Ford Bell Technical Center in Minneapolis, Minnesota, here's what you might expect:

The company describes its environment as "hands-on," with research employees actively involved in a broad spectrum of activities, including new product strategy, concept development, product formulation, process development, and scale-up and plant start-ups. Research and development personnel are the primary force in driving a project from the initial concept stage, through the development of prototypes, to testing and refinement, and to large-scale production and appearance on the grocer's shelves. In the role of innovator, project leader, and technical problem solver, you team up with General Mills' marketing, marketing research, manufacturing, and sales professionals. Together you are accountable for expanding new product businesses and making major product improvements.

At General Mills, research and development focuses on product and process development and on long-term applied research projects. As an entry-level food scientist or chemical, food processing, or packaging engineer, you'll develop and maintain the systems, processes, and, most importantly, the products that keep General Mills among the top competitors. You could play a critical role in a new product start-up or participate in a research program that helps the company target long-term strategic objectives.

A degree in food science, food technology, chemistry, biochemistry or chemical, food process, or packaging engineering is a requirement in research and development, with a preference for master's or doctoral degrees.

Meet Art Davis, Ph.D.

Dr. Davis is Director of Scientific Services at the American Association of Cereal Chemists, where he has served for the past two years. He obtained his bachelor's degree at Oregon State University and spent two years in the Peace Corps. Then he went on to graduate school at Kansas State University, where he earned a master's and a Ph.D. in cereal chemistry. "I knew I was always headed into biology and the sciences," he says.

After working for Pillsbury Company in their research and development department, he assumed a position heading a research group for the American Institute of Baking for about two and one-half years. Following that, he served on the faculty of Kansas State University for nine years. Subsequent positions included quality assurance manager for General Foods Bakeries and three years as the director of technical services for the Green Giant Fresh Vegetables Group.

"Here, at the American Association of Cereal Chemists, the main thing we do is offer about thirty short courses and other continuing education programs," Dr. Davis explains. "Whenever there's a need to provide basic information in food science, we fill that void. For instance, there's been a tremendous growth in the use of frozen foods in this country in the last six or seven years, and a lot of (particularly smaller) companies are interested in getting into that field. Since there was no training available, we went out and found some people who were knowledgeable about this topic and put together a two-day course that provides the basics to those who need this information.

"Other courses include water activity, wet miling sensory analysis, food technology, batter and breading technology, chemical leavening, breakfast cereal technology, chemistry technology, and principles of cereal science. Individuals often come to us with biology, microbiology, or engineering backgrounds but no experience with food. So for individuals both overseas and here in the states, our courses provide the information needed.

"Another service we provide is an international check sample service. Every month, bimonthly, or quarterly, samples are sent to participating laboratories. They then perform a specific analysis and send us their findings. We then compile all of the results and provide a report that reveals the findings of perhaps a hundred labs. This gives the labs some idea of whether they are in line with other labs and how accurate their findings are. In fact, this year we're starting to do some proficiency certification. If you send all of the samples in for a year and your results are in line with the other labs, we'll issue you a certificate verifying that.

"Because there's a critical size that must be reached before it's feasible to have your own research and development group, smaller companies tend to depend on their suppliers to do their research ad development for them. For instance, my experience at the General Foods Bakeries taught me that you can mix doughnut batter in your plant, starting with flour, sugar, salt, and so forth, but because of some of the peculiarities of putting doughnut mixes together, it's a lot more efficient to buy a mix from a company that makes doughnut mixes. If you've got a problem with it, you ask them to solve it, or if you want something a little bit different, you ask them to create that for you. Flavor houses, mix suppliers, and fats and oils suppliers have their own research and development divisions, as do some of the bakers and mills. These are the people who can get you the properties you want, and they'll go out in their labs and massage the molecules until they come up with what you desire.

"For those interested in getting into food science, I would highly recommend Kansas State University's Department of Grain Science and Industry. They've got three curricula there: milling, baking, and seed plants (which has to do with building animal feeds). The undergraduate program, which includes serious chemistry, physics, and a little bit of engineering, is so excellent that every student that graduates from there has at least a couple of job offers. There is also a graduate program, and they never have any trouble placing those people either.

"Minnesota has a small but growing program in the cereals area through their food science department. Iowa State has a little bit. Texas A & M has a couple of people who do pretty good work. It's not labeled food science—I think it's crop and food science. There are some other schools, but Kansas State, Minnesota, Texas A & M, and Iowa State are probably the primary ones. Then at the graduate level, Kansas State and North Dakota State University have good graduate programs and A & M's got a grad group that works in cereals as does Iowa State. Just drop a line to those universities and see if their programs are of interest to you.

"If you are planning on doing research at a university, I'd recommend that you get a Ph.D. However, industry doesn't get terribly hung up on degrees. I know a number of good researchers with master's degrees who have gone on and done quite well. I even know of a few with bachelor's degrees who have distinguished themselves. If you are an able researcher, there are opportunities out there for you."

PLANT SCIENCE

Plant science is another important area of agricultural science. Contained within it are agronomy, entomology, crop science, plant breeding, horticulture, and some others.

Scientists performing this specialty study plants, plant growth, soil characteristics, and everything else related to plant health. Their aim is to aid those who produce food, feed, and fiber crops to most efficiently and effectively feed a huge population. At the same time much thought is given to maintaining the environment and conserving our natural resources. Both productivity and nutritional value are of the utmost importance. Some crop scientists study breeding, physiology, and management of crops and use the tenets of genetic engineering to create crop species that are hardier and more resistant to disease. Utilizing observation techniques and intensive study, scientists develop new crop varieties, raise the quantity and quality of existing species, and enhance the crops' resistance to drought and pests.

An example of work in plant science might be the production of a new plant species as a result of using hybridization, a process whereby two different plant breeds are "crossed" to produce a new strain (which carries the best of both parent plants).

Meet George Ware, Ph.D.

Dr. Ware served as research director at the Morton Arboretum in Illinois for more than twenty years. The Morton Arboretum is a multifaceted facility that boasts an active research program along with a herbarium and library. Under their Research Associates Program, the Arboretum gives scientists who are working on plant projects a place to perform their work. The arrangement is of mutual benefit because the Arboretum receives the advantage of up-to-date information and the scientists are able to make use of a convenient workplace and have the cooperation of a staff. Ware says that, "This takes us to the heart of the mission of research—to find better answers and convey them in language the public can understand. Through our Research Associates Program we are able to disseminate sound information that we ourselves have generated rather than relying upon other references entirely."

The Arboretum was established in 1922 by J. Morton, founder of Morton Salt. Particularly slanted to a Chicago-area focus, the Arboretum seeks to maintain a regional approach to its work.

With more than 4,000 kinds of trees and shrubs, the Arboretum has learned which trees have a short life, which are likely to contract specific plant diseases, and which don't do well in direct sunlight. All of this information is happily given to the public, so everyone gains from the work done here.

Recent projects at the Arboretum include a project to determine the amount of root loss trees can withstand as a result of construction activities and another that involves the use of a gas chromatograph (provided by Amoco Research Corporation), which will help measure salt deposits in the soils at the Arboretum and other areas in the region.

SOIL SCIENCE

It is the responsibility of soil scientists to study the physical, biological, chemical, and mineralogical composition of soils as all of these properties relate to the growth of plants or crops. This means that they are involved in ascertaining the responses of various soil types to fertilizers, crop rotation, and tilling practices. Responses are gathered through observation, study, and scientific testing.

Soil scientists who are employed by the federal government often conduct soil surveys. This means that they classify and map the soils they find. With this in hand, they are able to provide suggestions and information to farmers and others who grow plants. Recommendations may be made regarding the optimum use of their land, how to improve the productivity of the plants, and the best ways to avoid a variety of problems such as erosion.

Sometimes history teaches us that we have had to learn things the hard way. Nineteenth-century Americans are held responsible for the enormous erosion damage to parts of Mississippi, Tennessee, and the Piedmont plantation region. As a result the Soil Survey was set up in 1899. Following that and the devastation of the dust bowl storms, the United States government established the Soil Conservation Service in 1933 to help farmers in their quest to make the best possible use of their land.

Soil scientists may work in any of the following four areas: survey, conservation and management, crop production, and soil productivity.

Scientists working in conservation and management are involved in helping to determine the best use of land. They may also be given projects that focus on the control of erosion and water quality. Those who work in soil surveys map and classify the best use of land. The category of soil science work may be dictated by the soil scientist's position and the type of facility he or she is positioned at.

Consultations with other technical personnel and perhaps engineers who are working on construction projects may be required. The close relationship between soil science and environmental science sometimes means that experts in soil science may also be called upon to use their knowledge to ensure environmental quality and intelligent use of land. Soil and crop scientists can also expect to spend at least a portion of their time outside conducting research on farms or agricultural research stations.

Soil scientists who wish to work in private industry may be required to meet specific qualifications and successfully complete an examination. Soil technicians are usually required to have completed a minimum of thirty hours in physical science, earth science, or biology (with fifteen hours in soils).

Soil scientists may be employed by the Soil Conservation Service, the Environmental Protection Agency, the United States Department of Agriculture, and the United States Department of the Interior.

ANIMAL SCIENCE

Animal scientists are devoted to finding and developing improved methods of producing and processing meat, poultry, milk, and eggs. This is accomplished by poultry scientists, dairy scientists, and animal breeders through the study of genetics, reproduction, nutrition, and growth and development of domestic farm animals.

Poultry scientists study breeding, feeding, and management of poultry in an effort to improve both the quantity and quality of eggs and other poultry products. Dairy scientists are involved in the study of dairy cattle to uncover how environment and feed affect the production and quality of milk. Their responsibilities include developing breeding programs and improving dairy herds. Other duties will include anything that affects the livestock, such as disease control, sanitation, and the physical accommodations of the animals.

Some scientists work to understand how the animals' environment affects their behavior, how their treatment affects the quality of the meat, and other behavioral studies such as why a few animals take on leadership roles.

Some animal scientists are responsible for inspecting and grading livestock, purchasing livestock, or working in marketing or technical sales. Others work as extension agents, who act as consultants to agricultural producers helping them to increase production of products like milk and to best address other matters of importance to them.

Animal scientists are responsible for developing pigs and beef cattle that have less fat and more muscle, dairy cows that produce more milk, and chickens that lay more eggs. But more than quality and quantity are involved in the researcher's work. They seek more humane ways to raise animals and processes that are more economical and more efficient. As a result they need to study diseases, sanitation, housing, and other concerns related to animals.

Some animal scientists are animal nutritionists—specialists who study how foods make animals grow.

Meet H. Graham Purchase

Dr. Purchase presently serves as Director of Veterinary Medical Research at Mississippi State University.

Born in Rhodesia (now Zimbabwe), Dr. H. Graham Purchase was educated in Kenya, East Africa, and then received his university training in South Africa. "My father, also a veterinarian who worked in research, always said that since animals feed on plants, it's wise to learn about the plant world before going to veterinary school." So Dr. Purchase went to college when he was sixteen and earned a bachelor's degree in botany. He then completed his veterinary degree in South Africa, practiced for two years, and then fulfilled his dream of coming to the United States to do research. While employed here, he earned a master's and a Ph.D. at Michigan State University majoring in microbiology and public health. "It took eight years to complete the Ph.D.," he says, "but it was well worth it."

"I started my research in a poultry lab in East Lansing, Michigan, and after a few years here, met an American girl, married her, and decided to become a citizen. I worked at the poultry research lab for about thirteen years doing research on tumor viruses of poultry. And here is one occasion where I can say I was definitely at the right place at the right time because the laboratory discovered the cause of one of the most economically devastating poultry diseases of the world (Marek's disease, a form of cancer) and created a vaccine that would prevent it. The first commercial applicable cancer vaccine ever developed, it was initially patented and used in the United States extensively. Now it's used worldwide. This period was the most exciting and rewarding of my life," he says.

"As a 'bench' researcher, I examined the cultures of cells in which we grew the viruses that cause disease or the vaccine that prevented the disease. Routinely I would go to the necropsy room and find those birds that had died in the experiments. I would open those birds and examine what they died from to make sure it was the challenge that they died from and not something that didn't relate to the experiment. The rest of the day would involve writing up manuscripts and grant proposals. Often, writing was taken home to complete because I many times couldn't get it done during the daytime hours.

"After thirteen years, I moved up into administration and was offered a job in Washington, DC. I spent fourteen years there in nine different jobs in research administration. The research was in a variety of areas: plant, animal, human, nutrition, family economics, soil, and water. But I have a great interest in veterinary research, and when the opportunity presented itself here at Mississippi State in the College of Veterinary Medicine, I took it. Here we do research on the prime commodities of Mississippi, which include one of our big income producers—catfish— and our number-one product—poultry.

"As a research administrator, a typical day here involves interacting with many individuals one-on-one. I handle the budget of the college, so often there are budget forms, various commitment forms to sign; for example, allowing people to travel, allowing people to buy new equipment, allowing people to be hired. There are also manuscripts and proposals to review to make sure they're suitable. We are accredited by the American Association for the Accreditation of Laboratory Animal Care, and they have very high standards of review for all experiments on animals. Every single experiment that involves animals has to be reviewed by an animal care and use committee to make sure that the animals are not harmed unnecessarily. Also the accreditation involves making sure that the facilities are maintained, so that is another area of concern for me.

"A good part of my day is devoted to meetings with my superiors to inform them about how the research projects are progressing. Frequently I have visitors to escort through our research facilities. I have reports to prepare on the research that we are doing, most of which are lay reports for general use for administrators and the legislators. The actual writing up of the research itself is done by the faculty. We have a system where a faculty member writes the manuscripts and proposals and they get sent out for peer review to make sure they are well written, to make sure that the conclusions are supported by the data, and so on. I orchestrate that review process.

"We have many levels of researchers working here. Generally speaking, the principal investigators or leaders, the ones who actually design the experiments, have a Ph.D. But we also have a variety of other types of careers involved. We have a lot of technicians; some have master's degrees, some have bachelor's degrees. We have animal caretakers and animal technicians; some of them have technician degrees, others are just high school graduates. We have quite a number of students working toward bachelor's degrees who get some experience in the field by doing lab clean-up work here. Then we have grad students and individuals who already have their bachelor's degrees who are going on to get their master's or Ph.D. degrees. These students spend a good deal of the time with their major professors learning how to conduct experiments and do research, so that when they graduate they'll know how to perform these tasks independently.

"If you're grades are good, if you perform well during examinations, and if you can become an expert in these areas, research is a wonderful career. It's challenging, it's very innovative. I enjoy the ability to develop new things and to find out new things. But it's very rigorous, too. Most of my researchers are not here from nine to five. They're here early in the morning, they frequently miss their lunches, and they take work home at night or come in at night and weekends to keep their work going. Research means pushing forward the frontiers of science, and to succeed, you must be trained, prepared, and dedicated to putting in the necessary hours and effort."

EDUCATION AND TRAINING

High school students should follow a prescribed college entrance curriculum including English, mathematics, science (particularly biology, physics, and chemistry), foreign language, and social science classes.

The requirements for agricultural scientists vary depending on the specialty and the kind of work they do. For some jobs in applied research, a bachelor's degree in agricultural science may be sufficient. However, usually a master's or doctoral degree is necessary to work in basic research. Those who wish to teach (and do research) at the college level must earn a Ph.D. in agricultural science. This would also be true for those who have set a goal to advance to an administrative research position. Those who obtain a degree in a related science such as physics, chemistry, or biology, or certain engineering specialties may also be qualified for jobs in this field.

Agricultural science degrees are offered by at least the one land-grant college found in every state. In addition numerous other colleges offer agricultural science degrees or a least course work in that area.

Requirements in this field usually include the following: life and physical science courses, business, communications, economics, and a wide choice of technical agricultural science classes. This would depend on the chosen specialty. For instance, a candidate for animal science might take nutrition, reproductive physiology, and animal breeding. Someone seeking a specialty in food science would take food microbiology, food chemistry, food analysis, and a course in food processing operations. Someone interested in soil science might take entomology, plant physiology, biochemistry, plant pathology, and soil chemistry. If you are leaning toward an advanced degree, expect to be performing fieldwork, classroom work, laboratory research, and a thesis based upon your independent research.

Planned curricula in animal science offers varied courses including biology, genetics, microbiology, physiology, chemistry, nutrition, and some other sciences. Additional course work is often recommended in economics, research methods, physics, mathematics, and statistics.

At the advanced level, courses like animal production, management, breeding, and behavior will be offered along with food science, endocrinology, and related subjects. Advanced degrees are usually attained through a combination of fieldwork and laboratory research in addition to classroom assignments. A doctoral thesis will be necessary for all doctoral candidates.

For food scientists minimum standards for undergraduate college programs have been set by The Institute of Food Technologists (IFT). In addition to biology, nutrition, chemistry, statistics, and physics, students must also take food analysis, food microbiology, food engineering, and food analysis. Also helpful are classes in business management economics and marketing, particularly for those interested in a career in business or industry.

In order to be accepted as a member of The Institute of Food Technologists, you must have a minimum of a bachelor's degree in food science or a related field and five years of professional experience. The organization also has an active membership for students.

Though most people may think of a scientist working independently in a lab or in the field, you may be surprised to learn that it is important to be able to work effectively as a team member. More often than not you will be required to operate efficiently with others as the member of a team.

Another important skill area is that of communication. Agricultural scientists must be able to communicate effectively both orally and in writing. After all, what good is performing research and making new discoveries if you cannot convey this information to others in an understandable and meaningful way? Additionally, perseverance, curiosity, accuracy, diligence, and patience are desirable qualities.

WORKING ENVIRONMENT

Agricultural scientists usually work in offices and laboratories. Some may work outside as part of the fieldwork necessary to conduct their observations and experiments. Those working for the government, cooperative extension programs, or other agencies may travel.

Some animal scientists work in labs but others work in offices, research stations, feedlots, or stockyards. In the field they may study the animals, conduct tests, and analyze their results.

EMPLOYMENT

Approximately 29,000 individuals work as agricultural scientists. In addition to this, several thousand serve as faculty members in agricultural science positions at numerous colleges and universities.

Many agricultural scientists are employed by federal, state, or local governments. Nearly 30 percent work for the federal government, mostly the Department of Agriculture. Large numbers also work for state governments, at state agricultural colleges or agricultural research stations. Some are employed by agricultural service companies, some by commercial research and development laboratories, seed companies, food products companies, wholesale distributors, botanical gardens and arboretums, and pharmaceutical concerns. In addition, a substantial number are self-employed and serve mainly as consultants. Agricultural scientists may perform research and development themselves or serve in the capacity of managers or administrators in food production companies or companies that produce machinery, supplies, or chemicals.

Animal scientists with master's degrees may be hired to work on practical applications of basic research findings to specific agricultural problems. Areas may include breeding, animal nutrition, physiology, and animal environments.

Animal scientists employed by a federal or state research station may find themselves spending time at farm animal facilities or dairies or outside conducting livestock research. In federal positions, animal scientists may be hired by the U.S. Public Health Service, Food Safety Inspection Service, Animals and Plant Health Inspection Service, the U.S. Department of Agriculture, or the Food and Drug Administration.

Advancement is possible for those who enter as staff members in a research lab. Once experienced, they may progress to research on more intricate projects. Executive positions will be available to those who have both scientific and managerial experience. Some animal scientists become specialists in their chosen area, for instance, nutrition or genetics.

Job Prospects

The United States Department of Labor's *Occupational Outlook Handbook* predicts that employment of agricultural scientists will grow about as fast as the average for all occupations through the year 2005. For animal scientists the prospect is excellent through the year 2005.

Opportunities will be available in all of the subfields of agricultural science, particularly for soil scientists with an environmental interest; plant and animal scientists with a molecular biology, genetics, biotechnology, or microbiology specialty; and food technologists.

You may expect that those with advanced degrees will have the best opportunity to find employment. However, teaching positions at the university level will be difficult to come by even for doctoral holders. This is because federal and state budgets may limit funding through 2005.

Those who hold bachelor's degrees may find employment in research and product development, usually in areas such as food science and technology. The federal government also hires bachelor's degree holders to operate as soil scientists for the Soil Conservation Service. A bachelor's degree is also useful for managerial jobs in businesses that deal with farmers and ranchers; feed, seed, fertilizer, or farm equipment manufacturers; farm credit institutions; retailers; or wholesalers. Undergraduate degrees may also provide an entrance to the fields of cooperative extension service agent, technician, landscape architect, farmer or farm manager, or purchasing or sales agent for agricultural supplies.

PROFESSIONAL ASSOCIATIONS

A number of organizations promote the interests of agricultural scientists. They include the American Dairy Science Association, the Poultry Science Association, the American Farm Bureau Federation, the American Horticultural Society, American Society for Horticultural Science, Soil Science Society of America, the American Society of Animal Science, and the American Meat Science Association. For entomologists the largest is the Entomological Society of America (ESA), with approximately 8,000 members.

SALARIES

According to the College Placement Council, graduates with a bachelor's degree in animal science received beginning offers averaging $22,000 annually. An average salary for all federal employees in animal science was about $49,000 per year. Animal scientists in private industry often receive higher salaries. Graduates in plant science averaged $22,150.

The United States Department of Labor's *Occupational Outlook Handbook* reveals that salaries for federal positions in nonsupervisory, supervisory, and managerial positions averaged the following: agronomy, $45,911; animal science, $55,631; soil science, $43,033; horticulture, $44,492; and entomology, $53,889.

Median salary for food scientists is approximately $34,000. Those with a bachelor's or master's degree should expect to start at about $21,000 to $24,000 per year. Those with experience and a bachelor's or master's degree may earn $37,000. Doctoral degree holders can earn $42,000 a year.

Food scientists with bachelor's degrees who are employed by the federal government might expect about $16,000 to $21,000. Master's degree holders will range from $20,000 to $26,000. Those with doctoral degrees will range from $25,000 to $32,000.

FOR ADDITIONAL INFORMATION

Information on federal job opportunities may be found at local state employment security agencies or offices of the U.S. Office of Personnel Management, found in most major metropolitan areas. Additional information is available from the following sources:

American Horticultural Society
P.O. Box 0105
Mount Vernon, VA 22121

American Institute of Baking
  1213 Bakers Way
  Manhattan, KS 66502

American Society of Agronomy
  Crop Science Society of America
  Soil Science Society of America
  677 South Segoe Road
  Madison, WI 53711

The American Society of Animal Science
  309 West Clark Street
  Champaign, IL 61820

American Society for Horticultural Science
  701 North Saint Asaph Street
  Alexandria, VA 22314

Food and Agricultural Careers for Tomorrow
  Purdue University
  1140 Agricultural Administration Building
  West Lafayette, IN 47907-1140

Institute of Food Technologists
  Suite 300
  221 North LaSalle Street
  Chicago, IL 60601

Interstate Publishers, Inc.
  P.O. Box 50
  Danville, IL 61834

National FFA Organization
  P.O. Box 15160
  Alexandria, VA 22309

Office of Higher Education Programs
  U.S. Department of Agriculture
  Room 350A, Administration Building
  Fourteenth Street and Independence Avenue, SW
  Washington, DC 20250

Soil Conservation Service
    Fourteenth Street and Independence Avenue, SW
    Washington, DC 20013

Soil Science Society of America
    677 South Segoe Road
    Madison, WI 53711

United States Department of Agriculture
    Soil Conservation Service
    Public Information
    Washington, DC 20050

Young Entomologists' Society, Inc.
    1915 Peggy Place
    Lansing, MI 48910-2553

CHAPTER 4

THE PHYSICAL SCIENCES

Research is formalized curiosity. It is poking and prying with a purpose.

—Zora Neale Hurston, *Dust Tracks on a Road* (1942)

We can thank physical scientists for the advances in solid-state physics (the science of crystals, minerals, and metals), which has led to revolution after revolution in the microelectronics industry. Innovations such as lasers, fiber optics, megabit microchips, particle beams, medicines, paints, plastics, and cancer radiation therapy are all directly attributable to physical scientists.

Within the world of physical science, there are many divisions. They include:

CHEMISTS

Chemists make contributions to the world around them by being problem solvers. They seek out information about chemicals and then put these discoveries to practical use. Their work is based upon the premise that all physical things, (natural or man-made) are made up of chemicals. So they investigate the structure, properties, and composition of matter and create, or further develop, products or processes. To this end, they focus on the laws that control the combination of elements and the reactions that occur as a result of these joinings. They are also responsible for developing processes that save energy and reduce pollution, such as petrochemical processing methods.

In the area of applied research, chemists use the information gleaned from basic research to compose new products or improve those already in existence. For instance, basic research on the process of polymerization (combining of small molecules to form larger ones) resulted in the development of synthetic rubber and plastic products.

Like most sciences, chemistry consists of a number of subfields. Four of the major ones include the following:

Analytical chemistry. This field is devoted to finding out the exact composition of substances.

Organic chemistry. This field concentrates on compounds containing carbon and studies the ways carbon combines with other substances. Organic compounds are produced by living things. Fields that may contain opportunities for employment include wood products, plastics, foods, textiles, and petroleum.

Inorganic chemistry. This field focuses on compounds that contain no carbon. In the mining industries, they seek avenues to break down ores to retrieve pure metals and minerals, and in the electronics industry, they work on development of such things as methods of building solid-state electronic components such as integrated circuits.

Physical chemistry. This field studies the physical properties of matter.

Further subfields include agricultural chemists who study the chemical action of soils, plants, insects, animals, and so forth, in relationship to agriculture; food chemists who analyze frozen, canned, and cooked foods to ensure quality; and polymer chemists who work with plastics and elastomers (rubberlike substances).

GEOLOGISTS AND GEOPHYSICISTS (EARTH SCIENTISTS)

Geologists and geophysicists are involved in the study of our planet Earth. They focus on investigating the materials of which the Earth is made, the processes that act upon these materials, the products formed, and the history of the planet and its life forms since the beginning of time. Using a combination of fieldwork and laboratory or office work, they gather data by identifying and examining rocks, creating maps, studying the remains of fossils, examining physical and chemical properties of laboratory specimens, studying information provided by sensing instruments like seismographs, conducting geological surveys, and using instruments to measure the Earth's gravity and magnetic field. This is accomplished through the use of compasses, hammers, pocket lenses, barometers, microscopes, cameras, survey equipment, and a variety of other instruments.

Employment in geoscience may be found in a wide variety of businesses and fields including the petroleum industry, state and federal government agencies, and education. Geologists may also provide advice in the construction of buildings, dams, highways, and tunnels.

Geologists and geophysicists often begin their careers in field exploration or as research assistants in laboratories. They are given more difficult assignments as they gain experience. Eventually they may be promoted to project leader, program manager, or other management or research positions.

One of the fastest growing areas in geoscience involves protecting and restoring the environment. This includes issues such as hazardous waste and water quality and availability.

Some subcategories of Earth science include:

Geochemists who analyze the composition of Earth materials.

Geophysicists who use quantitative means to study physical properties of the Earth.

Oceanographers who study the marine environment in the oceans, including physical, chemical, biologic, and geologic aspects.

Hydrologists who study the distribution, circulation, and physical properties of underground and surface waters.

Petroleum geologists who explore for oil and gas.

Mineralogists who analyze the chemical properties of deposits, precious stones, and mineral rocks.

Paleontologists who study the chronology of the history of the Earth through fossil plants and animals.

Stratigraphers who help locate minerals by studying the distribution and arrangement of sedimentary rock layers and by examining the fossil and mineral content of such layers.

Environmental geologists who design pollution control systems and waste disposal sites.

Volcanologists who study volcanoes.

Seismologists who study earthquakes and other similar activity.

Aeronomists who study the upper atmosphere.

Geodesists who study the shape, size, weight, and changes in the Earth's shape.

Geomagneticists who focus on the Earth's magnetic field.

METEOROLOGISTS

Scientists involved in meteorology study the atmosphere's physical qualities and also the effect that the atmosphere has on our environment. The most commonly known application of this information is predicting both day-to-day and long-range weather. However, weather information and meteorological research are also applied in other areas such as agriculture, air and sea transportation, defense, global warming or ozone depletion, and air-pollution control.

Several subcategories of meteorologist include:

Synoptic meteorologists who analyze weather information from satellites and specially equipped worldwide stations.

Operational meteorologists or *weather forecasters* who forecast the weather for the general public and also specialized groups such as agriculture, marine, or aviation.

Physical or research meteorologists who perform research on atmospheric physics, creating and improving mathematical models of atmospheric processes and events. They work in laboratories and in the field studying severe storms, weather modification, and new methods of predicting weather.

Climatologists who study, collect, organize, interpret, and publish weather information they have gathered over long periods of time.

Instrumentation specialists who develop instruments and systems to measure and record the variables of weather.

Consulting meteorologists who provide forecasts specifically geared for industry, business, or government.

Dynamic meteorologists who focus on the movement of weather systems and the forces that control them.

Other specialized fields include hurricane forecasting, satellite meteorology, spaceflight meteorology, fire weather forecasting, radar meteorology, and mathematical analysis and programming.

PHYSICISTS

In broad terms, physicists are involved in the study of nature—all natural phenomena not covered by biology and chemistry. In a more specific manner, physics is the study of matter, energy, and the interactions between the two. This encompasses the study of force and motion (mechanics), sound (acoustics), heat (thermodynamics), electricity and magnetism, and light (optics).

Most physicists work either in basic research to increase scientific knowledge or in applied research to devise new processes, techniques, and products. Physicists who engage in applied research build upon the discoveries already accomplished by basic researchers in an attempt to develop new devices, products, and processes. For instance, basic research in solid-state physics led to the development of transistors, which, in turn, led to the development of integrated circuits used in computers.

Physicists also design research equipment that often has additional unanticipated uses. For example, lasers are now used in surgery, microwave devices are used for ovens, and measuring instruments can analyze blood or the chemical content of foods.

Most physicists specialize in one of many subfields: atomic and molecular physics, elementary particle physics, plasma physics, and nuclear physics. Some may specialize in a further subdivision of one of these subfields, for example, within condensed matter physics, specialties include superconductivity, crystallography, and semiconductors. Also, growing numbers of physicists work in combined fields such as biophysics, chemical physics, and geophysics.

One of Ronald Reagan's last actions as president was to approve the decision to go ahead with the Superconducting Super Collider, a multi-billion-dollar project for particle physics research, to be built in Waxahatchie, Texas, during the 1990s. The purpose of this was to keep American physics at the cutting edge of research.

ASTRONOMERS

Astronomy deals with the entire universe outside of the Earth. Although, in large measure, it is based upon physics, it is quite different from physics because of one crucial factor—it is not possible to do actual laboratory experimentation in astronomy because in most cases we can only observe from a distance. Thus astronomy uses optics and electromagnetism to gather information.

Almost all astronomers perform research. They analyze large quantities of data gathered by observatories and satellites and write scientific papers or reports on their findings. Examples of fields of research in astronomy include studies of stellar atmospheres, planetary atmospheres, properties and composition of interstellar materials, and cosmology (the structure, history, and future evolution of the universe). An astronomer might study how the stars and planets formed, how the galaxy evolved as it did, and how new stars may form.

One of the major milestones of modern astronomy was the launching of the Hubble Space Telescope into orbit. This telescope is much more sensitive than a ground-based telescope and has provided us with pictures and information we would never have had otherwise.

Astronomers often concentrate their studies on one particular subspecialty such as:

Astrophysicists who focus on stars; how they function and how they change as they age.

Cosmologists who study the properties and evolution of the observable universe.

Radio astronomers who use sensitive telescopes to study the source and nature of celestial radio waves.

Solar astronomers who study the sun.

EDUCATION AND TRAINING

High school students interested in the physical sciences should concentrate on courses like biology, chemistry, physics, and mathematics. Four years of mathematics including trigonometry, calculus, and computer experience is desirable. English, public speaking, and foreign languages are also recommended.

More than 600 colleges and universities are approved by the American Chemical Society and about 325 institutions also offer advanced degree programs in chemistry.

Chemistry

Individuals working towards bachelor's degrees in chemistry should expect to take courses in analytical, inorganic, organic, and physical chemistry. General course work will also include physics, biology, mathematics, and liberal arts classes. Foreign languages such as German, French, or Russian are worthwhile because many technical manuscripts useful for research are written in these languages. Computer programming is also a plus.

At the graduate level, scientists usually focus on a particular specialty. Each one calls for a great deal of laboratory research. Although graduate students typically specialize in a subfield of chemistry, such as analytical chemistry, students usually need not specialize at the undergraduate level. In fact, undergraduates who are broadly trained may have more flexibility when job hunting or changing jobs than if they narrowly define their interests.

Some employers provide new bachelor's degree chemists with additional training or education. A master's degree will take two years of full-time studies. A doctoral degree will require three to five years of additional study beyond a bachelor's degree.

It's important to be intelligent, curious, detail-minded, and have the ability to work with abstract concepts. Since chemists often work on interdisciplinary teams, they need the ability to get along with others, some understanding of other disciplines, leadership ability, and good oral and written communication skills. Experience, either in academic labs or through internships or co-op programs in industry, is also useful.

In general, those with bachelor's degrees may work as research assistants, product testers, or sales representatives. Master's degrees are necessary for applied research positions and some teaching jobs in community colleges. Doctorates are usually required for administrative or supervisory positions in industry, for teaching at the university level, or in government or industrial research.

Geology and Geophysics

More than 500 colleges and universities offer bachelor's degrees in geology, geophysics, oceanography, and other geosciences. More than 300 offer advanced degrees in these fields.

Traditional geoscience courses emphasizing classical geologic methods and concepts, such as mineralogy, paleontology, sedimentary geology, petrology, field geology, mineralogy/crystallography, stratigraphy, and structural geology, and other laboratory courses are important for all geoscientists. However, those students interested in working in the environmental or regulatory fields should take courses in hydrology, hazardous waste management, environmental legislation, chemistry, fluid mechanics, and geologic logging.

For geologists or geophysicists, a Ph.D. is essential for most college or university teaching positions, and is important for work in federal agencies that involve basic research. Geoscientists working for the government may study a number of important subjects from local land-planning needs to the updating of topographical maps and other research topics. General geology or Earth science is most often selected as the undergraduate major. Next most common are petroleum engineering and geophysics. At the graduate level most masters' degrees are in geophysics, general geology/Earth science, or petroleum engineering. Most doctoral degrees are in geophysics, economic/mining geology, or petroleum engineering.

Geologists and geophysicists need to be able to work as part of a team. Computer modeling, data processing, and effective oral and written communication skills are also important, as well as the ability to think independently and creatively. Those involved in fieldwork must have physical stamina.

Meteorology

Because meteorology is a small field, relatively few colleges and universities offer degrees in meteorology or atmospheric science, although many departments of physics, Earth science, geography, and geophysics offer atmospheric science and related course work. Prospective students should make certain that courses required by the National Weather Service and other employers are offered at the college they are considering. Computer science courses, additional meteorology courses, and a strong background in mathematics and physics are expected to become more important to prospective employers as new, sophisticated weather equipment and radar systems become operational. Many programs combine the study of meteorology with another field, such as agriculture, engineering, or physics. For example, hydrometeorology, the blending of hydrology (the science of the Earth's water) and meteorology, is an emerging field concerned with the impact of precipitation on the hydrologic cycle and the environment.

The preferred education requirement for entry-level meteorologists in the federal government is a bachelor's degree, not necessarily in meteorology, with specific semester hours in meteorology courses. Also calculus and physics at the college level are required. These requirements will probably be upgraded soon and most likely will include course work in computer science and additional course work appropriate for a physical science major, such as statistics, chemistry, physical oceanography, or physical climatology. A master's degree is usually necessary for conducting research and development and a Ph.D. for college teaching.

Physics and Astronomy

About 750 colleges and universities offer a bachelor's degree in physics. The undergraduate program provides a broad background in the natural sciences and mathematics. Typical physics courses include mechanics, electromagnetism, optics, thermodynamics, atomic physics, and quantum mechanics.

About 180 colleges and universities have physics departments that offer Ph.D. degrees in physics. Graduate students usually concentrate in a subfield of physics such as elementary participles or condensed matter.

Those with bachelor's or master's degrees in physics are usually qualified to work in an engineering-related area or other scientific field, to work as technicians, or to assist in setting up laboratories. Some may qualify for applied research jobs in private industry or nonresearch positions in the federal government. Masters' degrees are often sufficient for teaching jobs in two-year colleges, but, overwhelmingly, research positions require doctoral degrees.

About 72 universities offer the Ph.D. degree in astronomy, either through an astronomy department, a physics department, or a combined physics/astronomy department. Applicants to astronomy doctoral programs face keen competition for available slots. Those planning a career in astronomy should have a very strong physics background; in fact, an undergraduate degree in physics is excellent preparation, followed by a Ph.D. in astronomy.

Mathematical ability, computer skills, an inquisitive mind, imagination, and the ability to work independently are important traits for anyone planning a career in physics or astronomy. Prospective physicists who hope to work in industrial laboratories applying physics knowledge to practical problems should broaden their educational background to include courses outside of physics, such as economics, computer technology, and current affairs. Good oral and written communication skills are also becoming increasingly important.

Most Ph.D. physics and astronomy graduates choose to take a postdoctoral position, which is helpful for those who want to continue research in their specialty and for those who plan a career teaching at the university level. Beginning physicists, especially those without a Ph.D., often do routine work under the close supervision of more senior scientists. After some experience is gained, they are assigned more complex tasks and given more independence. Physicists who develop new products or processes sometimes form their own companies or join new firms to exploit their own ideas.

People having training in astronomy with B.S. or M.S. degrees may find employment in applied areas, such as spaceflight mission planning, as assistants to research astrophysicists at observatories, universities, and government labs.

WORKING ENVIRONMENT

In most cases physical scientists work a typical forty-hour week. However, when focusing on a project, researchers may be called upon to work additional hours.

Chemists and physicists work in well-equipped laboratories performing experiments and also put in considerable hours in offices doing theoretical research, planning, recording, and reporting on their lab research. However, experiments in plasma, nuclear, high energy, and some other areas of physics require extremely large, expensive equipment such as particle accelerators, which may only be available in certain laboratories. Thus, traveling may be required. Other physical scientists spend time outside collecting the specimens they need to examine. They usually conduct their work in teams with co-workers and other scientists and professionals. In order to avoid injuries, those who work with caustic materials wear masks, gloves, glasses, and other gear.

Geologists and geophysicists may work overseas or in remote areas. Geological and physical oceanographers may spend considerable time at sea.

Astronomers may need to travel to observatories, which are usually in remote locations, and work routinely at night.

EMPLOYMENT

Of the approximately 92,000 chemists in the United States, 60 percent work for manufacturing firms mostly in the chemical manufacturing industry, which includes drugs, soaps, and synthetic materials companies. About 19,000 of these are employed in college teaching and research and about 9,000 work for state and local governments. Federal employers include the U.S. Departments of Defense, Agriculture, the Interior, and Health and Human Services.

Although positions for chemists are available all over the United States, the greatest numbers of openings exist in and around large industrial centers such as New York, Philadelphia, and Chicago. States with the most chemists include California, Illinois, Ohio, Pennsylvania, and New Jersey.

Geologists and geophysicists hold about 48,000 jobs. This is not counting the large number of people who hold faculty positions in colleges and universities. Many work for the Department of the Interior in the U.S. Geological Survey, the Bureau of Land Management, the Minerals Management Service, the Bureau of Mines, and the Bureau of Reclamation. Others work for the Departments of Defense, Agriculture, Commerce, and Energy and the Environmental Protection Agency (EPA).

The largest employer of civilian meteorologists is the National Oceanic and Atmospheric Administration (NOAA), which employs about 2,400 meteorologists. The majority of NOAA's meteorologists work in the National Weather Service at stations in all parts of the United States. The remainder of NOAA's meteorologists work mainly in research or program management. The Department of Defense employs about 280 civilian meteorologists. Others work for private weather consultants, research and testing services, and computer and data processing services. In addition to civilian meteorologists, thousands of members of the armed forces do forecasting and other meteorological work.

There is a large concentration of research meteorologists in Boulder, Colorado; Kansas City, Missouri; Cincinnati, Ohio; Norman, Oklahoma; Las Vegas, Nevada; Miami, Florida; Idaho Falls, Idaho; Oak Ridge, Tennessee; Raleigh, North Carolina; and Princeton, New Jersey.

Approximately 32,000 physicists are employed in all sections of the United States with the largest numbers in industrial areas and large research and development laboratories. Private industry employs physicists in basic and applied research on electrical and electronic devices and scientific instruments. Federal agencies employ about 20 percent of all physicists. These include labs associated with or funded by the U.S.

Department of Defense, the National Aeronautics and Space Administration, the U.S. Department of Commerce, and the U.S. Department of Energy.

There are about 21,000 physicists and astronomers. This is not counting college and university instructors. About 40 percent of all nonfaculty physicists work in research, development, and for testing laboratories in the industry. The federal government employs about 20 percent, mostly in the Departments of Defense and Commerce and in the National Aeronautics and Space Administration (NASA). Others may work in colleges and universities in nonfaculty positions and for aerospace firms, noncommercial research laboratories, electrical equipment manufacturers, engineering services firms, and the transportation equipment industry. Although physicists are employed all over the United States, most work in areas that have universities and large research and development laboratories.

Job Prospects

Outlook for most physical scientists through the year 2005 is expected to grow about as fast as the average for all occupations. Job prospects look best for those in pharmaceuticals and biotechnological industries. Employment in private manufacturing will remain strong due to the continual development of new products.

However, employment will not grow as quickly as in the past because, overall, research and development budgets are expected to grow more slowly compared with those of the 1980s, as firms restructure and streamline their operations.

A large proportion of physicists and astronomers are employed on research projects, many of which, in the past, were defense related. Expected reductions in defense-related research and an expected slowdown in the growth of civilian physics-related research will cause employment of physicists and astronomers to decline through the year 2005. Since the number of doctorates granted in physics is not expected to decrease much from present levels, competition is expected for the kind of research and academic jobs that those with new doctorates in physics have traditionally sought.

Although research and development budgets in private industry will continue to grow, many research laboratories in private industry are expected to reduce basic research, which is where much physics research takes place, in favor of applied research and product and software development. Furthermore, although the number of retiring academic physicists is expected to increase in the late 1990s, it is possible that many of them will not be replaced or will be replaced by faculty in other disciplines.

PROFESSIONAL ASSOCIATIONS

The American Chemical Society sets guidelines for the education and training of undergraduates in chemistry and publishes a list of schools that comply with their guidelines. The National Certification Commission in Chemistry and Chemical Engineering awards certification to chemists and chemical engineers who stay current in the field. Other groups include the American Association for Clinical Chemistry, The American Institute of Chemists, and the Association of Official Analytical Chemists.

For geologists and geophysicists, the largest organization is the American Geological Institute, which represents member societies with a combined enrollment of 80,000. Other options include the Society of Exploration Geophysicists with about 16,000 members, the American Geophysical Union with about 25,000 members, the Society of Exploration Geophysicists, the American Geological Institute, the Association for Women Geoscientists, and the Geological Society of America.

For meteorologists, the American Meteorological Society (AMS) with 1,500 members and the National Weather Association (NWA) with 2,200 members are popular.

The American Institute of Physics is an association that consists of ten societies and eighteen affiliated societies. The largest member society of the American Institute of Physics is the American Physical Society, which boasts a membership of about 43,000 members, most of whom are research physicists. For astronomers there is the American Astronomical Society with 5,100 members, the Astronomical Society of the Pacific with 7,000 members, and the International Astronomical Union, which includes astronomers from all over the world.

SALARIES

The College Placement Council reports an average starting salary of about $27,000 for graduates with a bachelor's degree in chemistry. Those with a master's degree averaged $32,000, doctoral degree holders averaged approximately $48,000 per year.

The American Chemical Society reports that the median salary of their members at all experience levels with a bachelor's degree was $44,000 a year; with a master's, $52,000; and with a Ph.D., $65,000.

Chemists in nonsupervisory, supervisory, and managerial positions in the federal government earned an average salary of $51,500 according to the *Occupational Outlook Handbook*.

A survey by the College Placement Council revealed that graduates with bachelors' degrees in the geological sciences received starting offers of about $26,000. The American Geological Institute reports average starting salaries for inexperienced geoscientists to be about $23,000 with a bachelor's degree, $29,000 for those with a master's degree, and $34,000 for those with a Ph.D. However, there are wide industry differences. For instance, the oil and gas industries offered larger salaries than research institutions and colleges and universities.

The average salary for meteorologists in nonsupervisory, supervisory, and managerial positions employed by the federal government averages around $49,000. Meteorologists in the federal government with a bachelor's degree and no experience can expect about $20,000 to $23,000 per year, depending on their college grades. Those with a master's degree could start at about $25,000 to $28,000, those with a Ph.D. degree at about $35,000 to $41,000.

According to the College Placement Council, starting salaries for physicists average about $30,000 per year for those with a bachelor's or master's degree, and about $41,000 for those with a doctoral degree. The College Placement Council reports that graduates with a bachelor's degree in physics received starting offers averaging about $22,000 per year. Those with a master's degree received offers averaging about $32,000 a year, and those with doctorates averaged about $51,000 per year. The American Institute of Physics reports a median salary of $65,000 for its Ph.D. credentialed members. Average salaries for physicists in nonsupervisory, supervisory, and managerial positions in the federal government averaged about $62,000 per year. For astronomy the figure was about $66,000.

FOR ADDITIONAL INFORMATION

Additional information is available from the following sources:

American Association for Clinical Chemistry
Education Department
2029 K Street NW, Seventh Floor
Washington DC 20036

American Association of Petroleum Geologists
Communications Department
P.O. Box 979
Tulsa, OK 74101

American Astronomical Society
Education Office University of Texas
Department of Astronomy
Austin, TX 78712-1083

American Chemical Society
Education Division
1155 Sixteenth Street, NW
Washington, DC 20036

American Geological Institute
4220 King Street
Alexandria, VA 22302-1507

American Geophysical Union
2000 Florida Avenue NW
Washington, DC 20009

American Institute of Physics
1 Physics Ellipse
College Park, MD 20740

American Meteorological Society
45 Beacon Street
Boston, MA 02108-3693

American Physical Society
American Center for Physics
1 Physics Ellipse
College Park, MD 20740

Geological Society of America
P.O. Box 9140
3300 Penrose Place
Boulder, CO 80301

Michigan Technological University
Office of Admissions
1400 Townsend Drive
Houghton, MI 49931

National Weather Service
Personnel Branch
1335 East-West Highway, SSMCI
Silver Spring, MD 20910

Taylor & Francis Publishers, Inc.
1900 Frost Road, Suite 101
Bristol, PA 19007

CHAPTER 5

ENGINEERING

(Scientists) are peeping Toms at the keyhold of eternity.

—Arthur Koestler, *The Roots of Coincidence* (1972)

Engineering is recognized as one of the oldest careers in the world. And it is the one responsible for Roman roads, plastics, pharmaceuticals, fuels from crude oil, Spanish ships, and the creation and development of industry and space programs in the United States.

More than twenty-five major specialties are now recognized by professional societies. They include the following:

CHEMICAL ENGINEERS

Chemical engineers apply the principles of chemistry as well as those of mathematics, engineering, and physics to seek means for mass production of chemical products such as medicines, synthetic fibers, and plastics. Often they specialize in a particular operation such as oxidation or polymerization or a particular area such as pollution control or the production of a particular product such as chlorine bleach. Many chemical engineers work in the aircraft, manufacturing, or electronics industries. High-demand specialties that fall within the chemical engineering sphere include health and safety management, environmental work, and automated process control.

The industries into which chemical engineering graduates are traditionally hired are enjoying some of their best years ever. These industries include petrochemicals and plastics, where growth rates are rising as are profits. The pulp and paper industry continues to run at maximum capacity. Health care and cosmetics are also growing at a rapid rate, boosted by the commercial entry of products from the biotechnology industry.

A report from the National Academy of Engineering, published with the partial sponsorship of the American Institute of Chemical Engineers, details current research and development needs for chemical engineering technology. The list includes: biochemical and biomedical engineering; electronic, photonic, and recording materials and devices; advanced materials; energy and natural resources processing; environmental protection, safety, and hazardous materials; computer-assisted process and control engineering; and surface and interfacial engineering.

AEROSPACE ENGINEERS

The field of aerospace engineering is a combination of two fields: aeronautical (atmospheric-flight) engineering and astronautical (space flight) engineering. Engineers working for aerospace companies may work in a wide range of engineering specialties, which include:

Experimental engineers. These researchers build, test, and check models and prototypes for aerodynamics, stability and control, propulsion, and performance of the structures.

Propulsion engineers. These researchers design, modify, and test the power plant that makes the aircraft, rocket, or spacecraft move. Aerospace engineers work with the airflow in and out of the engine as well as the performance of the engine. Other engineers deal with the combustion chemistry, the electronic controls, or the mechanical design of the propulsion device.

Structural engineers. These researchers deal with stress, weight, and strength. The craft must be strong enough to carry the load for which it is intended, but not so heavy that its own weight reduces the payload. Structural engineers use electromechanical instruments to test full-scale models for their resistance to stresses such as those from wind, temperature, and shock. They may test the craft in real or simulated flight. Mechanical engineers skilled in stress analysis may also work on these structures.

Engineers in stability and control. These researchers work to make the aircraft fly easily. The control surfaces of aircraft and space vehicles are designed to permit the vehicles to fly safely through turbulence and wind shear. In spacecraft, the control surfaces prevent the overheating of the craft on reentry into the atmosphere. The design of the stability and control systems of high performance aircraft permits the craft to fly faster, turn quicker, and take off and land vertically or in a very short distance. Digital control systems enhance the performance of aerospace systems.

Materials engineers. These engineers are involved in deciding the material for each section of the aircraft. Any aircraft or spacecraft must have a high ratio of strength to weight, and resistance to heat and cold. Materials engineers decide what processes, such as heat treating or plating, will make materials usable without destroying useful properties.

The work of aerospace engineers focuses on several stages: The first is on preliminary design and advanced design, which considers the purpose of the aircraft or the system and the environment in which it will operate. Working with engineers in aerodynamics, stability and control, structures and materials, and propulsion systems (piston, rocket, or jet), they organize data and decide on possible shapes, sizes, arrangements of parts, and materials for the craft and its components. Then these ideas are translated into drawings or computer-aided designs. Through computer graphics, engineers can test the performance of their designs. It takes several years to take the idea from the drawing board to production. And, many times in between, things go back to the drawing board for changes.

Research and development in aerospace technology has produced a body of knowledge that is useful for much more than flight systems. Engineers and scientists use technologies developed for space flight to find new sources of energy and to make better use of natural resources. Aerospace engineers also design high-speed ground transportation, power units, guidance systems, underseas vehicles, controls for air and water pollution, biomedical instrumentation, and noise control systems. In addition they develop hydraulic, electrical, and electronic systems and devices that go into aircraft, missiles, and spacecraft. These instruments control flight, communications, and the equipment that records and transmits data to Earth.

In general, aerospace engineers who work for large aircraft manufacturing firms or in government research do not need to be registered. All fifty states and the District of Columbia require registration for engineers whose work may affect life, health, and property or who offer their services to the public.

Candidates for registration must have a degree for completion of an accredited engineering program and four years of relevant work experience. They may then be required to take a state examination.

DRYDEN FLIGHT RESEARCH CENTER

The Dryden Flight Research Center is considered NASA's premier installation for aeronautical flight research. Located at Edward's Air Force Base in California on the western edge of the Mojave Desert, the center is celebrating its fiftieth anniversary in 1996. Dryden has grown from an initial group of five engineers in 1946 to a facility with more than 460 NASA government employees and about the same number of civilian contractor personnel.

In addition to carrying out aeronautical research, the center also supports the space shuttle program as a primary and backup landing site, and as a facility to test and validate design concepts and systems used in development and operation.

Many recent projects have led to major advancements in the design and capabilities of many military and civilian aircraft. Since the days of the X-1, the first aircraft to fly faster than the speed of sound, the installation has grown in size and significance and is associated with many important milestones in aviation—supersonic and hypersonic flight, wingless lifting bodies, fly-by-wire, supercritical and forward swept, and the space shuttles.

While Dryden is working on a large number of diverse projects, perhaps the most visible is the space shuttle. The center was the site of the space shuttle Approach and Landing Tests (ALT) in 1977. The prototype orbiter *Enterprise* was used in ALT to verify the glide and handling qualities of the vehicle following its return into the atmosphere from space. During ALT, *Enterprise* was taken aloft atop the NASA 747 Shuttle Carrier Aircraft and air launched for the glide flights back to the lake bed and to the main runway at Edwards.

Dryden pilots and engineers were testing and validating design concepts that helped in the development of the space shuttle configuration more than a decade before testing began with the *Enterprise*. Subsequent flight testing at Dryden also contributed significantly in the development of the space shuttle thermal protection system, solid rocket booster recovery system, flight control system computer software, and the drag chutes designed to help increase landing efficiency and safety.

Since the first orbital flight in April 1981, the majority of landings have been at Dryden. After the landings the orbiters are serviced at Dryden for the ferry flights back to Kennedy Space Center in Florida piggyback atop the NASA 747 Shuttle Carrier Aircraft.

Meet Mary Shafer

Mary Shafer is a senior aerospace research engineer at Dryden Flight Research Center.

"As a high school student in the early sixties, I attended a National Science Foundation course at UCLA between my junior and senior years," says Shafer. "The subject happened to be meteorology, but it gave me a chance to see that science and research provided a way to explain the world around me, which I felt was interesting and important. Then I got a summer job working for the air force and discovered that I liked being near airplanes. I began my college career at UCLA as a chemistry major, but later switched to engineering. I spent subsequent summers working for NASA where I decided I truly loved airplanes and flight research. And I was very lucky. I had a lot of good people to work with, a lot of people willing to explain things to me, give me examples in everyday life that related to aerodynamics and fluid mechanics.

"During the summers at NASA, I began by reducing data, working with a ruler in engineering units, plotting the information on graph paper with orange carbon behind it. I wrote a couple of little programs, which impressed everybody because at that point very few people could do that. The next year I progressed to writing computer matrix manipulations designed to measure trial time stability analysis during flight, and that was really interesting because then I started to understand the rules that governed how airplanes flew.

"I got my bachelor's degree and came back and worked another summer writing quality programs for some of the engineers. Then I went back and got my master's degree. The next summer I was writing with engineers and proceeded to marry one. I came out of school under the Brooks Bill as a computer programmer writing follow-up programs for the X-24B, then worked for Lockheed on the FA certification of the L1011 and for McDonald Douglas and McDonald Aircraft, then worked on the F4 airplane and the initial acceptance testing of the F-15, and then to the air force as a systems designer working on writing programs. Then I came back over to NASA and got a job as a controls engineer.

"NASA employs aeronautical engineers, mechanical engineers, electrical engineers, meteorologists, and physicists. We cover a broad range of disciplines: engineering and the hard sciences, chemistry, physics, meteorology, math. It's important that you know math; it's extremely important that you know how to program and use the computer. The other thing you need to know is how to write clearly and grammatically. There's no point in doing research if you don't write it down clearly and well enough that people understand what you did, how you did it, why you did it, and what happened when you did it. Flexibility is another important quality for researchers because you don't know how your attempts are going to come out, and you have to be able to build upon your successes or shift gears when the outcome isn't as you'd planned. People who are unable to deal with uncertainty may find that research is not a good field for them. And in this line of work, a robust ego is a nice thing to have.

"Essentially right now I'm working on one particular experiment called the *aerospy,* and it's my responsibility to look at the various flying qualities to make sure that the modifications made to the airplane are safe and that we will be able to fly the airplane confident that it is structurally sound. Most of my day is spent at computers, sometimes talking with pilots, going down to the simulation area to see how it flies, watching the input of our new ideas, what our computer looks like, what the airplane looks like with the new lift and the new drag, etc. Then we put those in the simulator, and then the pilots fly it to see if it's going to fly well. For example, we figure out things like are we going to have enough runway to take off? Are we going to have enough thrust? Will it go forward instead of falling out of the sky? I'm also working on a number of smaller flying qualities research projects.

"My other real interest is how the aircraft pilot system works and what the pilot needs to get from the airplane to feel that it's a good airplane or a bad airplane. Tolstoy once said in his opening sentence to Anna Karenina, 'All happy families are alike, but each unhappy family is unhappy in its own way.' Well, the same is true of airplanes, a good airplane is not very interesting to your quality engineer, but a bad airplane is fascinating.

"I work fairly regular hours. However, it's my understanding that this is somewhat less common in the university setting. The situation here is that we'll occasionally have a surge of work. For instance, I've got to write a paper by November and so I'll probably do that on weekends, but then I'll go back to a normal work schedule.

"Research is essentially a neutral endeavor. When you begin a project, you never really know what will be gained, what you'll find out, and certainly how that information might be used. In later stages you will learn how the information gained from your research will affect, and hopefully benefit, the world we live in."

Meet LTC Joseph W. McVeigh

McVeigh is chief of the operations division of the U.S. Army's Airworthiness Qualification Test directorate.

The army has a small group of officers (approximately 2,000) from the ranks of captain to colonel that make up the Acquisition Corps. These officers come from all of the branches of the army (armor, infantry, aviation, field artillery, and so forth). The purpose of the Acquisition Corps is to have an elite group of officers that procure all of the equipment, weapons, vehicles, that the army requires for its operations. This includes research and development, test and evaluation, program management, and staff/support functions.

"For clarification, the army differentiates between research and development (R & D) and test and evaluation (T & E)," says McVeigh. "I'm not sure if they are considered one and the same in the civilian world. The research and development personnel work in the army laboratories and at universities doing basic research and concept exploration. I work in the T & E area. We do the developmental testing of hardware (testing to specs) and operational testing (testing with troops to determine operational suitability—does it work the way it's supposed to?).

"I've always wanted to fly, and I decided the best way to do this was to join one of the armed services. I went to the University of Montana in Missoula because it was convenient and inexpensive (my parents lived there). Air force and army ROTC were located there and were always ready to welcome a new cadet. I joined army ROTC during my sophomore year, completed school, and received a B.S. degree in forestry in 1979. [McVeigh subsequently received an M.A. degree in computer resource management from Webster University in St. Louis, Missouri.] Once I graduated and got commissioned as a second lieutenant, I was off to Fort Knox, Kentucky, for the Armor Officers Basic Course. While at the Basic Course, I applied for flight school and was accepted. While I was at my first flying assignment following flight school, I was selected to support an aviation test for a new type of radio. The test lasted three months and after it was over, I realized this is what I wanted to do in the army. Although the test organization I was supporting (the Aviation Board, Ft. Rucker, Alabama) was small (thirty officers), I was lucky enough to get assigned there.

"My previous jobs (T & E and R & D related) include test project officer, where I conducted operational tests on several aircraft-related components, and UH-60 plans officer where I initiated test plans for operational testing for future programs. Both of these jobs were done while I was at Ft. Rucker as a Captain. When I moved to the aviation systems command in St. Louis, I performed as an aeronautical engineer working on the design of various cockpits to provide human factors input on design, layout, safety-of-flight critical items, etc. (one year). My second job (one and a half years) in St. Louis was doing administrative type work for two general officers. My third job (two years) was coordinating joint programs with the navy and air force so that we all worked toward using the same equipment in the future. I also worked with Canada, England, and Saudi Arabia to initiate joint laboratory type work between those countries and the army.

"Currently, I'm stationed at Edwards Air Force Base with the U.S. Army Airworthiness Qualification Test Directorate where they conduct airworthiness flight testing of army helicopters and airplanes. When I first arrived I performed as a flight test engineer on several tests, including work on the OH-58D helicopter and the MH-47E helicopter.

"As a flight test engineer, I was in charge of the flights. I told the experimental test pilots what profile to fly, how to fly it, and for how long. Designing the test plan was one of my major responsibilities. It was the road map that everyone would follow to conduct the test. I also coordinated the flight crews and crash rescue crews, test budgets, and personnel overtime.

"On a typical day as a flight test engineer, I would come in at 07:00 and pick up where I had left off on reducing data from the previous day's (or week's) flights. If a test flight was scheduled for that day for my aircraft, I briefed the crews, maintenance personnel safety and crash rescue, and flight operations personnel on what we were doing and the schedule for the day. I would then coordinate the aircraft's preparation for the flight (if it wasn't done the previous afternoon). My responsibilities also included preparing the flight data card, operating all the test equipment and data recording equipment on board, and queuing the pilots as to what to do next during the flight.

"If I didn't have a flight going that day but someone else did, I would fly a chase aircraft alongside them as they flew their profile (for safety). The chase pilot coordinates the airspace and makes all the radio calls to ground and air traffic control and range control.

"I remained in that job for one year and then was selected for my current position as chief of the operations division. I and the people under me are in charge of the organization's budget, flight operations, photography and graphic arts support, technical publications support, and business office. In addition I fly in support of flight tests here and at other remote sites that we have jurisdiction over.

"This type of career requires people who are dedicated to their work, who want to provide the world with something better than what they already have."

ELECTRICAL AND ELECTRONICS ENGINEERS

Electrical and electronics engineers are part of the largest field of engineering at present, the branch of physics that deals with electricity and magnetism. The electrical/electronic engineer applies basic engineering principles, both electrical and mechanical, in designing and creating electric power generation and transmission systems, computers, communications systems, computer hardware, video equipment, automatic control systems, and other electrical equipment.

Electrical and electronic engineers are part of most aspects of modern technology and scientific research, including health and medicine, transportation, and aerospace.

Some specialties of electrical and electronics engineers include:

Solid-state electronics. The branch dedicated to working with devices such as silicon, which are of great importance to electronic systems.

Computer electronics. The branch devoted to creating systems that can process more data in less time with operators needing less training and expertise.

Other specialties include transmission, telecommunications, power systems, distribution, and electrical equipment manufacturing.

BIOMEDICAL ENGINEERS

Biomedical engineers research, design, and develop instruments, devices, and procedures to diagnose, monitor, and treat illnesses or ailments. The field called biomedical engineering is a combination of engineering expertise and medical needs for the enhancement of health care. It is a branch of engineering in which knowledge and skills are developed and applied to define and solve problems in biology and medicine. Students choose the biomedical engineering field to be of service to people, for the excitement of working with living systems, and to apply advanced technology to the complex problems of medical care. The biomedical engineer is a health care professional, a group that includes physicians, nurses, and technicians. Biomedical engineers may be called upon to design instruments and devices, to bring together knowledge from many sources to develop new procedures, or to carry out research to acquire knowledge needed to solve new problems.

Examples of work done by biomedical engineers include:

- Designing and constructing cardiac pacemakers, defibrillators, artificial kidneys, hearts, blood oxygenators, blood vessels, joints, arms, and legs.
- Designing computer systems to monitor patients during surgery or in intensive care, or to monitor healthy persons in unusual environments, such as astronauts in space or underwater divers at great depth.
- Designing instruments and devices for therapeutic uses, such as a laser system for eye surgery or a device for automated delivery of insulin.
- Implementing new diagnostic procedures, especially those requiring engineering analyses to determine parameters that are not directly accessible to measurements, such as in the lungs or heart.
- Developing strategies for clinical decision making based on expert systems and artificial intelligence, such as a computer-based system for selecting seat cushions for paralyzed patients, for managing the care of patients with severe burns, or for diagnosing diseases.

Specialty areas include bioinstrumentation, biomechanics, biomaterials, systems physiology, clinical engineering, and rehabilitation engineering.

Biomedical engineers are employed in industry, in hospitals, in research facilities of educational and medical institutions, in teaching, and in government regulatory agencies. They often serve a coordinating or interfacing function, using their background in both the engineering and medical fields. In industry they may create designs where an in-depth understanding of living systems and of technology is essential. In research institutions biomedical engineers supervise laboratories and equipment and participate in or direct research activities in collaboration with other researchers with such backgrounds as medicine, physiology, and nursing.

Some biomedical engineers also have advanced training in other fields. For example, many biomedical engineers also have an M. D. degree, thereby combining an understanding of advanced technology with direct patient care or clinical research.

NUCLEAR ENGINEERS

Nuclear engineering is one of the newest fields of engineering. It is an outgrowth of nuclear physics, which also includes several aspects of mechanical and other engineering disciplines.

Nuclear engineers are involved with the design, construction, and operation of nuclear power plants and fuel processing facilities. One major project is to develop a means of controlling thermonuclear fusion as a new source of power. Accomplishing this would mean that the heavy hydrogen (deuterium) in sea water could provide a nearly limitless, clean source of energy.

Some nuclear engineers work on the development of nuclear weapons; others explore the possibilities of finding industrial and medical uses for radioactive materials.

CIVIL ENGINEERS

Professionals in this field belong to the oldest branch of engineering. These specialists design and supervise the construction of large stationary structures such as roads, airports, tunnels, bridges, water supply structures, buildings, and sewage systems. Specialties within this field include water resources engineer, environmental engineer, construction engineer, transportation engineer, structural engineer, geotechnical engineer, hydraulics engineer, and soils engineer.

Other specialties include traffic engineering, highway engineering, sanitary engineering, and municipal engineering.

Three main employers of civil engineers include engineering consulting firms, construction companies, and government agencies.

INDUSTRIAL ENGINEERS

Industrial engineers analyze and plan ways to increase the efficiency of workers, materials, and equipment for the most effective production of goods and services in all types of industries. The bridge between management and operations, they are most concerned with increasing productivity through the management of people and methods of business organizations.

They select the processes and methods to be used in the manufacture of a product, decide the sequence of making the parts, and develop plant layouts for machinery. Industrial engineers also establish the standards for the performance of workers and appropriate wage scales.

MECHANICAL ENGINEERS

Mechanical engineering is the broadest engineering discipline, extending across many interdependent specialties. It is an outgrowth of the branch of physics known as mechanics, an area that deals with the motions and properties of solid bodies and fluids. Mechanical engineers are involved in the design and development of machinery that may generate power or use it by conversion into a more useful form. Examples of this would include steam and gas turbines, jet and rocket engines, automobiles, airplanes, trains, computer-aided design, manufacturing internal combustion engines, and robotics, to name a few.

The work of mechanical engineers varies according to the industry and function they perform. Specialties include the following:

Automotive engineers. These mechanical engineers are involved in the design of vehicles and engines for automotive products of the future.

Fluids engineers. These mechanical engineers specialize in the design and/or manufacture of fluid flow systems.

Heating, ventilation, and air-conditioning (HVAC) engineers. These mechanical engineers concentrate on designing heating, venting, air-conditioning, and refrigeration systems.

Manufacturing engineers. These mechanical engineers are involved with designing and updating machines or processes implemented in manufacturing every conceivable product from airplanes to paper towels.

Systems engineers. These mechanical engineers focus on the design and analysis of mechanical or thermal systems.

EDUCATION AND TRAINING

High school students interested in engineering should undertake an academic program that includes algebra, plane and solid geometry, calculus, trigonometry, general science, physics, chemistry, biology, social studies, history, and English. Courses in electronics, if available, and computer science will prove helpful. Laboratory experience is also important. Proficiency in a foreign language is strongly recommended. The high school preparation for biomedical engineering is the same as for any other engineering discipline, except that life science course work should also be included. Those thinking about an aerospace career should start no later than their third year of high school to learn what studies they will need for admission to college. A high grade point average and good scores on examinations such as the Scholastic Aptitude Test may be part of the college admission requirements.

About 400 colleges and universities offer a bachelor's degree in engineering and nearly 300 in engineering technology, although not all are accredited programs. Some of the institutions do not offer training in the smaller specialties. Also, programs of the same title may vary in content.

Bachelor's degree programs in engineering are typically designed to last four years, but many students find that it takes between four and five years to complete their studies. A typical college curriculum consists of the first two years of basic sciences (mathematics, physics, and chemistry), introductory engineering, the humanities, social sciences, and English. The last two years focus mostly on engineering courses, usually with a concentration in one branch. Some programs offer a general engineering curriculum; students then specialize in graduate school or on the job.

A few engineering schools and two-year colleges have agreements whereby the two-year college provides the initial engineering education and the engineering school automatically admits students for their last two years. In addition a few engineering schools have arrangements whereby a student spends three years in a liberal arts college studying pre-engineering subjects and two years in the engineering school and receives a bachelor's degree from each. Some colleges and universities offer five-year master's degree programs.

Some five- or even six-year cooperative plans combine classroom study and practical work, permitting students to gain valuable experience and finance part of their education.

At the college level, the biomedical engineering student usually selects engineering as a field of study, then chooses a concentration within engineering. Some students may major in biomedical engineering, while others may major in electrical, mechanical, or chemical engineering with a specialty in biomedical engineering.

Biomedical engineers must have at least a bachelor's degree in biomedical engineering for completion of a program accredited by the Accreditation Board for Engineering and Technology. Among studies for this career are biomedical engineering systems and design, biomedical computers, engineering biophysics, bioinstrumentation, biomechanics, biothermodynamics, biotransport, and artificial organs.

Some students enroll in a traditional engineering program as an undergraduate student and then go on to study biomedical engineering in graduate school. A master's or a doctoral degree is necessary for top research positions in industry and government laboratories. Completion of a master's degree program takes two years of full-time study. Students who decide to go for a doctorate choose a specialty in biomedical engineering and then carry out research in that subject.

Some universities that have both a medical school and an engineering school offer a combined M.D. and Ph.D. program to prepare students for careers in medical research.

Students should enroll in an aerospace engineering program accredited by the Accreditation Board for Engineering and Technology (ABET). This rating affirms the quality of the education students receive, and it also improves their chances of employment after they graduate. Accreditation is especially important for students who plan to continue their studies because graduate study is limited to those who have attended a college with an accredited program.

The first two years of an aerospace engineering program consist of basic physical and engineering sciences, mathematics, and nontechnical subjects. Studies include English, analytic geometry, calculus, physics or chemistry, engineering mechanics, and thermodynamics. In their third year students may choose a program stressing design or research and development. Subjects may include applied aerodynamics, structural analysis, metals and metallurgy, fluid mechanics, electromagnetic fields, and aeronautical laboratory. Other studies are flight vehicle design, vehicle stability and control, flight mechanics, trajectory dynamics, electronics, and aerospace propulsion systems.

Many colleges offer cooperative education programs in aerospace engineering. Students enrolled in these programs alternate classroom study with jobs in industry or government. Most of these programs require five years to complete. Students in these programs receive pay for the work they do, which ranges from 60 to 80 percent of the starting salary for engineers, and this helps them meet college costs. When they graduate, they already have one or two years of experience.

A bachelor's degree in engineering from an accredited engineering program is usually required for beginning engineering jobs. College graduates with a degree in a physical science or mathematics may occasionally qualify for some engineering jobs, especially in engineering specialties in high demand. Most engineering degrees are granted in branches such as electrical, mechanical, or civil engineering. However, engineers trained in one branch may work in another. This flexibility allows employers to meet staffing needs in new technologies and specialties in short supply. It also allows engineers to shift to fields with better employment prospects, or ones that match their interests more closely.

Graduate training is essential for engineering faculty positions but is not required for the majority of entry-level engineering jobs. Many engineers obtain a master's degree to learn new technology, to broaden their education, and to enhance promotion opportunities.

All fifty states and the District of Columbia require registration for engineers whose work may affect life, health, or property, or who offer their services to the public. Recent figures number about 380,000 engineers registered. Registration generally requires a degree from an engineering program accredited by the Accreditation Board for Engineering and Technology, four years of relevant work experience, and successful completion of a state examination.

Engineers should be able to work as part of a team and should have creativity, an analytical mind, and a capacity for detail. In addition engineers should be able to express themselves well, both orally and in writing.

WORKING ENVIRONMENT

Engineers may be expected to work in laboratories, offices, construction sites, or research laboratories. Usually they work a forty-hour week during typical daytime hours. However, longer hours may be necessary when working on an important project, to conduct tests, or in order to meet a deadline. They work at desks, drafting tables, and computer terminals and with research and test equipment.

Many chemical engineers work with dangerous chemicals that require special precautions. Engineers in flight testing often fly the test aircraft.

EMPLOYMENT

There are approximately 52,000 chemical engineers. Seventy percent work in the manufacturing industries, mostly in the chemical, petroleum refining, and related industries. Most of the remainder work for engineering services, independent consultants, government agencies, or research and testing services.

Aerospace engineers number about 66,000. About 55 percent are in the aircraft and parts and guided missile and space vehicle manufacturing industries. Federal government agencies, primarily the Department of Defense and the National Aeronautics and Space Administration, provide more than one out of ten jobs. Engineering and architectural services, research and testing services, communications equipment manufacturing firms, and business services account for most of the remainder. The largest number of aerospace engineers are employed in Washington, Texas, and California, which have the largest numbers of aerospace manufacturers. Other states with jobs for aerospace engineers include New York, Ohio, Connecticut, Massachusetts, Florida, Georgia, Kansas, Maryland, Missouri, Minnesota, and New Jersey.

There are about 73,000 aerospace engineers. About 66 percent work in industries that manufacture aircraft and parts, guided missiles, and space vehicles. About 10 percent of these professionals work for the federal government.

As employees of the U.S. Department of Defense, aerospace engineers work in research and test centers of the air force, army, and navy. They work for the National Aeronautics and Space Administration (NASA) and the Federal Aviation Administration (FAA). A few work for commercial airlines, consulting firms, and colleges and universities.

Electrical and electronics engineers belong to the largest engineering branch, numbering approximately 370,000. Most jobs are with companies that manufacture electrical and electronic equipment, business machines, professional and scientific equipment, and aircraft and aircraft parts. Some of these engineers are employed by computer and data processing services firms, engineering and business consulting firms, public utilities, and government agencies.

Currently there are about 4,000 biomedical engineers. Those with advanced degrees are most marketable. The federal government employs biomedical engineers in the Food and Drug Administration, the U.S. Department of Veterans Affairs, the National Institutes of Health, and the National Aeronautics and Space Administration. In research institutions biomedical engineers supervise laboratories and equipment and take part in or direct research activities. In government jobs biomedical engineers often test products and establish safety standards. In industry they often serve as technical advisors. Most jobs for biomedical engineers are in or near large cities.

Of the approximately 17,000 nuclear engineers, about 20 percent work for the federal government, research and testing services, and utilities. About 50 percent of all federally employed nuclear engineers are civilian employees of the navy, about a third work for the Nuclear Regulatory Commission, and most of the rest work for the Department of Energy or the Tennessee Valley Authority. Most nonfederally employed nuclear engineers work for public utilities or engineering consulting companies. Some are employed by defense manufacturers or manufacturers of nuclear power equipment

About 173,000 civil engineers work in the United States. Over 40 percent of them are employed by federal, state, and local government agencies. Over one-third are in firms that provide engineering consulting services, primarily developing designs for new construction projects.

Because their skills may be used in almost any type of company, industrial engineers are more widely distributed among manufacturing industries than other engineers.

Mechanical engineers number about 227,000. Over 60 percent work in the manufacturing industries. Of these, most are in the electrical equipment, machinery, transportation equipment, and fabricated metal products industries.

Job Prospects

Although employment in the chemical manufacturing industry is not projected to experience significant growth through 2005, chemical engineers should find favorable job opportunities. The number of positions arising from employment growth, which is anticipated to be as fast as average for all occupations, and the need to replace those who leave the occupation should be sufficient to absorb the number of graduates with degrees in chemical engineering plus other entrants.

Areas relating to the production of industrial chemicals, biotechnology, and materials science may offer better opportunities than other portions of the chemical industry. Much of the projected growth in employment opportunities is expected to be in nonmanufacturing industries, particularly service industries.

Employment of aerospace engineers is expected to grow more slowly than the average for all occupations through the year 2005 due to decreased expenditures for military aircraft, missiles, and other aerospace systems. Growth in the civilian sector, which needs to replace the present fleet of airliners with quieter and more fuel-efficient aircraft, is projected to be much slower than previously anticipated due to the financial problems of airlines.

Job prospects for electrical and electronics engineers is expected to be good through the year 2005. Most openings will occur from job growth and also the need to replace electrical engineers who choose other occupations or leave the labor force entirely. Employment in this engineering specialty is expected to increase about as fast as the average. The best opportunities will be in industrial sectors other than manufacturing. Increased demand by businesses and government for computers and communications equipment is expected to account for much of the projected employment growth. Consumer demand for electrical and electronic goods and increased research and development on computers, robots, and other types of automation should create additional jobs.

Because of decreased spending in the area of defense, layoffs of electrical engineers is a possibility, especially for those who fail to keep up with the rapid changes in technology.

Employment of nuclear engineers is expected to remain about the same through the year 2005. Despite the expected absence of growth, good opportunities for nuclear engineers should exist because the number of persons graduating with degrees in nuclear engineering is likely to be in rough balance with the number of job openings. Those openings will arise as nuclear engineers transfer to other occupations or leave the labor force.

Spurred by an expanding economy and population growth, employment of civil engineers is expected to increase about as fast as the average for all occupations through the year 2005.

Employment of industrial engineers is expected to grow about as fast as average for all occupations through the year 2005. Industrial growth, more complex business operations, and the greater use of automation in factories and in offices underlie the projected employment growth. Because the main function of an industrial engineer is to make a higher quality product as efficiently as possible, their services should be in demand in the manufacturing sector as firms seek to reduce costs and increase productivity through scientific management and safety engineering.

As in other engineering specialties, employment of mechanical engineers is expected to grow about as fast as the average for all occupations through the year 2005. However, many mechanical engineering jobs are in defense-related industries, and reductions in defense may cause fewer employment possibilities.

PROFESSIONAL ASSOCIATIONS

The primary organization for chemical engineers is the American Institute of Chemical Engineers, with a membership of about 58,000. Another group is the American Chemical Society, which has a membership of about 149,000 who are involved in all branches of chemistry.

Aerospace engineers may belong to professional groups such as the Institute of Aeronautics and Astronautics or the American Astronautical Society. The AAS is an association of about 1,500 members and is dedicated to the advancement of the astronautical sciences and spaceflight engineering. Members are professionals in astronautics with at least six years of related training and experience. The American Institute of Aeronautics and Astronautics has a membership of about 44,000 engineers, scientists, and students in the aerospace field.

The American Institute for Medical and Biological Engineering is an organization of twenty professional societies. The Biomedical Engineering Society has about 1,800 members and the Association for the Advancement of Medical Instrumentation has about 6,000 members.

SALARIES

Starting salaries for engineers with bachelor's degrees are significantly higher than starting salaries of bachelor's degree graduates in other fields. According to the College Placement Council, engineering graduates with a bachelor's degree averaged about $34,000 a year in private industry, those with a master's degree and no experience about $39,000 a year, and those with a Ph.D, $54,400. The average annual salary for engineers employed by the federal government in nonsupervisory, supervisory, and managerial positions is about $54,000.

The starting salary for chemical engineers with bachelor's degrees is about $35,000. Many experienced chemical engineers earn more than $75,000 per year.

According to *Scientific Manpower Comments,* the median pay for aeronautical engineers is about $57,000 per year. Top aerospace engineers in industry may command a yearly salary of $94,000 or higher.

Other average figures for those with a bachelor's degree and no experience include: biomedical engineers, $31,000; petroleum engineers, $40,679; mechanical engineers, $34,462; nuclear engineers, $34,447; electrical engineers, $33,754; materials engineers, $33,502; industrial engineers, $32,348; and civil engineers, $29,376.

FOR ADDITIONAL INFORMATION

Additional information is available from:

American Chemical Society
    Career Services
    1155 Sixteenth Street NW
    Washington, DC 20036

American Institute of Aeronautics and Astronautics, Inc.
    AIAA Student Programs
    The Aerospace Center
    370 L'Enfant Promenade SW
    Washington, DC 20024-2518

American Institute of Chemical Engineers
345 East 47th Street
New York, NY 10017

American Nuclear Society
555 North Kensington Avenue
LaGrange Park, IL 60525

American Society of Civil Engineers
345 East 47th Street
New York, NY 10017

The American Society of Mechanical Engineers
345 East 47th Street
New York, NY 10017

Biomedical Engineering Society
P.O. Box 2399
Culver City, CA 90231

Institute of Electrical and Electronics Engineers
1828 L Street NW, Suite 1202
Washington, DC 20036

Society of Biomedical Equipment Technicians
3330 Washington Boulevard, 4th Floor
Arlington, VA 22201

CHAPTER 6

COMPUTER, MATHEMATICAL, AND OPERATIONS RESEARCH OCCUPATIONS

Scientists, like game players, prefer to devise their own strategies, even though these depend on an assimilated, shared body of knowledge.

— S. E. Luria, *A Slot Machine, A Broken Test Tube: An Autobiography,* (1984)

COMPUTER SCIENCE

Computers—It's hard to imagine a world without them. As a result of new technologies, particularly in the past twenty years, our modern society has been almost deluged by a continual introduction of new products, both in computer hardware systems and software. The highly trained, skilled group of professionals who are responsible for these tremendous advances in computer technology include computer scientists, computer designers, systems analysts, computer product design engineers, and software designers.

The manufacturing of computer hardware includes all the components such as the CPU (central processing unit) and peripheral equipment such as disks, monitors, storage devices, tape drives, and printers. Computer software consists of the program or programs comprised of machine readable instructions that perform a logical sequence of functions, from maintaining a bookkeeping system to performing computer games.

Computer scientists, including computer engineers, conduct research, design computers, and discover and use principles of applied computer technology. Though they may perform many of the same duties as other computer professionals, their jobs are distinguished by the higher level of theoretical expertise they apply to complex problems and the innovative ideas for the application or creation of new technology.

The computer professionals who are employed by academic institutions work in areas from theory, to hardware, to language design, or to multidisciplinary projects, for example, developing and advancing uses for artificial intelligence (AI). Their counterparts in private industry work in areas such as applying theory, developing specialized languages, or designing programming tools, knowledge-based systems, or computer games.

Computer Designers

Designers in the computer industry are responsible for researching and developing new computer hardware products. They analyze data to determine the feasibility of a product, work with other research personnel to develop a detailed description of the product, and plan and develop experimental test programs to determine the success or failure of their designs.

Computer Product Design Engineers

Computer product design engineers work alongside designers. Together they are responsible for developing new computer hardware products. Engineers assist designers in the development of specifications, supervise other engineers, and actually build the hardware product.

Software Designers

Software designers are the researchers who create the operating systems that allow users to interface with the computer. In addition they create the software products that perform specific functions or applications such as word processing packages.

Systems Analysts (Systems Engineers)

Systems analysts define business, scientific, or engineering problems and design their solutions using computers. This process may include planning and developing new computer systems or devising ways to apply existing systems to operations still completed manually or by some less efficient method. Usually these systems involve the processing of data in some type of business environment. Systems analysts may design entirely new systems, including hardware and software, or add a single new software application to harness more of the computer's power.

Analysts, architects of the computer team, begin their work by meeting with various individuals who are involved in the project. For instance, the Internal Revenue Service might need a new system to process tax returns, but the auditors and accountants don't have the expertise to know what is needed. So they seek the aid of a systems engineer. Much time is devoted to clearly defining the goals of the system so that it can be broken down into separate programmable procedures. Analysts then use techniques such as structured analysis, data modeling, information engineering, and cost accounting to plan the system. Once the design has been developed, systems analysts prepare charts and diagrams that describe it in terms that managers and other users can understand. They may prepare a cost-benefit and return-on-investment analysis to help management decide whether the proposed system will be satisfactory in every way.

After this study is completed, the analyst translates the requirements of the existing system into the capabilities of a computer system. He or she then prepares specifications for a programmer to follow so the programmer may write the necessary programs to make the computer system function as required. Some organizations do not employ programmers; instead a single worker called a *programmer/analyst* is responsible for both systems analysis and programming.

Some analysts become involved with every conceivable type of system. A business systems analyst may work with accounts receivable, accounts payable, inventory, general ledger, payroll, or any other type of business system. A scientific or engineering systems analyst may work, for example, on a system that analyzes stresses on steel beams or a system that is designed to send a man to the moon.

Because of up-to-date information—accounting records, sales figures, or budget projections, for example—is so important in modern organizations, systems analysts may be instructed to make the computer systems in each department compatible with each other so that facts and figures can be shared. Similarly, electronic mail requires open pathways to send messages, documents, and data from one computer "mailbox" to another across different equipment and program lines. Analysts musts design the gates in the hardware and software to allow free exchange of data, custom applications, and the computer power to process it all. They study the seemingly incompatible pieces and create ways to link them so that users can access information from any part of the system.

Computer Programmers

Programmers write the computer programs that provide the instructions for the computer to know what to do. There are many different kinds of programmers, but they can be placed into two main categories: business programmers and scientific programmers. Business programmers write programs for business applications and scientific programmers write programs for scientific and engineering applications. In computer installations employing systems analysts, the programmer works from problem descriptions prepared by the systems analyst. These problem descriptions include a detailed list of steps the computer must follow to obtain the desired results. The list of steps is converted by the programmer into a series of coded instructions called a computer program.

MATHEMATICIANS

Mathematics is an important field in itself, but also a very critical tool for virtually all other scientific and technical occupations. The world of mathematicians is one in which numbers and symbols are used to study quantities and relations.

Mathematicians are involved in a variety of activities that range from the creation of new mathematical theories to the translation of scientific and management problems into mathematical terms. Computers are used extensively to analyze relationships among variables, solve complex problems, develop models, and process large amounts of data.

The work of mathematicians falls into two main categories:

1. Theoretical (pure) mathematics, which focuses on developing new principles and relationships between existing mathematical principles.
2. Applied mathematics, which uses mathematics to develop theories, techniques, and approaches to solve practical problems.

These categories are not sharply delineated and sometimes overlap.

OPERATIONS RESEARCH ANALYSTS

Operations research and management science are two terms that are used pretty much interchangeably to describe the same field—which is also sometimes called decision technology. Basically operations research is a scientific approach to analyzing problems and making decisions. It uses mathematics and mathematical modeling on computers to forecast the implications of various choices and zero in on the best alternatives.

Developed during World War II, operations research helped take the guesswork out of deploying radar, searching for enemy submarines, getting supplies where they were most needed, and the like. And following the war, numerous peacetime applications emerged.

Manufacturers used operations research to make products more efficiently, schedule equipment maintenance, and control inventory and distribution. Success in these areas led to expansion into strategic and financial planning and into such diverse areas as criminal justice, education meteorology, and communications.

Operations analysts always begin by learning everything they can about the problem at hand. In order to accomplish this, they talk with people involved in all aspects of it, soliciting their varying perspectives and needs and their input into the solution. They examine available data, separating that which is truly relevant from that which is not. And they focus on practical, workable results, making sure what they propose is not just a theoretically appealing model, but one that will function effectively in the real world.

At this point the operations research analysts present their reports to management along with recommendations based upon their findings. Once there is acceptance of the analyst's work, all parties work together for its implementation.

Operations research analysts use computers extensively in their work. They are typically highly proficient in database management, programming, and in the development and use of sophisticated software programs. Most of the models built by operations research analysts are so complicated that only a computer can solve them efficiently.

The type of problem they usually handle varies by industry. For example, an analyst for an airline would coordinate flight and maintenance scheduling, passenger-level estimates, and fuel consumption to produce a schedule that optimizes all of these factors to ensure safety and produce the most profits. An analyst employed by a hospital would concentrate on a different set of problems—scheduling admissions, managing patient flow, assigning shifts, monitoring use of pharmacy and laboratory services, or forecasting demand for new hospital services.

The role of the operations research analyst varies according to the structure and management philosophy of the firm. Some centralize operations research in one department; others disperse operations research personnel throughout all divisions. Some operations research analysts specialize in one type of application; others are generalists.

STATISTICIANS

Statisticians collect, analyze, and interpret the numerical results of surveys and experiments to help officials and professionals determine the best way to produce and interpret results in their work. The importance of statistics lies in the facts they reveal. A count of votes from a sample of the population, for instance, can predict winners in a national or local election. Statistics can estimate crop yields, predict population growth, evaluate the chances of success of a new detergent, forecast population growth, or measure the efficiency of treatment for diseases.

Statisticians usually concentrate in one of two specialties. Mathematical statisticians look at statistics as a tool to reveal information. They deal with concepts such as probability theory and experimental design. Applied statisticians plan data collection and analyze and interpret numerical data from experiments, studies, surveys, and other sources.

Most statisticians use sampling techniques. For example, in this method they take a sample of a part of the population to judge the characteristics of the whole population. Computers have expanded and enhanced the work of statisticians by reducing the number of manual calculations.

Business and industry use statistics to make plans. Figures on production can show how a firm is performing. They may point out ways to cut waste and add to profits. They may help management make decisions.

Statisticians are vital to scientific research. The polio vaccine was proved effective after a nationwide statistical study showed that those who got the vaccine were less likely to get polio. Psychologists, too, have learned much about intelligence from statistical studies.

An entry-level statistician, right out of college, will generally work as a junior member of a statistical team and will spend most of the time doing fairly repetitive tasks such as organizing and categorizing data. With more experience and additional training, a statistician may become a leader of a statistical team and work more closely with company managers and government officials who have posed the problems or raised the questions to be studied by the team. At this level the statistician will be involved in designing experiments and tests, analyzing and interpreting data, and making predictions and forecasts. Statisticians working in colleges and universities are usually involved in teaching or research.

Because statistics are used in so many areas, it sometimes is difficult to distinguish statisticians from specialists in other fields who use statistics. For example, a statistician working with data or economic conditions may have the title of *economist.*

EDUCATION AND TRAINING

High school students should complete all course work typically recommended for college entrance: algebra, geometry, trigonometry, biology, chemistry, physics, English, and social studies.

There is no universally accepted way to prepare for a job as a computer professional. Employers' preferences depend on the work being done. But one thing is for sure—prior work experience is very important. This is not to say that education is not valued. However, if you are a "computer genius," you might be able to succeed in this field without an advanced degree or perhaps any degree at all.

Computer Science

College graduates are almost always sought for computer professional positions, and, for some of the more complex jobs, persons with graduate degrees are preferred. Generally a computer scientist working in a research lab or academic institution will hold a Ph.D. or master's degree in computer science or engineering. Some computer scientists are able to gain sufficient experience for this type of position with only a bachelor's degree, but this is more difficult. Computer engineers generally have a bachelor's degree in computer engineering, electrical engineering, or math. Computer designers need a minimum of a bachelor's degree in computer science or engineering. However, a master's degree is preferred.

Computer product design engineers are required to have a bachelor's degree in computer science or engineering. At one time software designers were required to have a bachelor's or master's degree in computer science. But now experience is given a considerable amount of weight.

Systems Analysts

For a business environment, employers usually want systems analysts to have a background in business management or a closely related field. For scientifically oriented organizations, a background in the physical sciences, applied mathematics, or engineering is preferred. Many employers seek applicants who have a bachelor's degree in computer science, information science, computer information systems, or data processing. Regardless of the college major, employers look for people who are familiar with programming languages and have a broad knowledge of computer systems and technologies. Courses in computer programming or systems design offer good preparation for a job in this field.

To achieve the title of *systems analyst,* one must have years of experience in data processing. This job experience is necessary for the analyst to fully comprehend the system being studied.

Systems analysts must be able to think logically, have good communication skills, and like working with people and ideas. They often deal with a number of tasks simultaneously. The ability to concentrate and pay close attention to detail also is important. Although systems analysts often work independently, they also work in teams on large projects. They must be able to communicate effectively with technical personnel, such as programmers and managers, as well as with other staff who have no technical computer background.

Technological advances come so rapidly in the computer field that continuous study is necessary to keep skills up to date. Continuing education is usually offered by employers, hardware and software vendors, colleges and universities, or private training institutions. Additional training may come from professional development seminars offered by professional computing societies.

The Institute for Certification of Computer Professionals offers the designation Certified Systems Professionals (CSP) to those who have four years of experience and who pass a core examination plus exams in two specialty areas. The Quality Assurance Institute awards the designation Certified Quality Analyst (CQA) to those who meet education and experience requirements, pass an exam, and endorse a code of ethics. Neither designation is mandatory, but either may provide a job seeker a competitive advantage.

Mathematics

A master's degree in mathematics is sufficient preparation for some research positions, for teaching jobs in many junior or community colleges, and in some small four-year colleges. However, in most four-year colleges and universities, as well as in many research and development positions in private industry, a doctoral degree is necessary.

In the federal government, entry-level job candidates usually must have a four-year degree with a major in mathematics or a four-year degree with the equivalent of a mathematics major (twenty-four semester hours of mathematics courses).

In private industry, job candidates generally need a master's degree to obtain jobs as mathematicians. The majority of bachelor's and master's degree holders in private industry work not as mathematicians, but in related fields such as computer science, where they are called computer programmers, systems analysts, or systems engineers.

A master's degree in mathematics is offered by most colleges and universities. Mathematics courses usually required for this degree are calculus, differential equations, and linear and abstract algebra. Additional course work might include probability theory and statistics, mathematical analysis, numerical analysis, topology, modern algebra, discrete mathematics, and mathematical logic. Many colleges and universities urge or even require students majoring in mathematics to take several courses in a field that uses or is closely related to mathematics, such as computer science, engineering, operations research, a physical science, statistics, or economics. A double major in mathematics and either computer science, statistics, or one of the sciences is particularly desirable.

About 255 colleges and universities offer a master's degree as the highest degree in either pure or applied mathematics; 187 offered a Ph.D. in pure or applied mathematics. In graduate school students conduct research and take advanced courses, usually specializing in a subfield of mathematics. Some areas of concentration are algebra, number theory, real or complex analysis, geometry, topology, logic, and applied mathematics.

For work in applied mathematics, training in the field in which the mathematics will be used is very important. Fields in which applied mathematics are used extensively include physics, engineering, and operations research; of increasing importance are computer and information science, business and industrial management, economics, statistics, chemistry, geology, life sciences, and the behavioral sciences.

Mathematicians should have substantial knowledge of computer programming because most complex mathematical computation and much mathematical modeling is done by computer.

Mathematicians need good reasoning ability and persistence in order to identify, analyze, and apply basic principles of technical problems. Communications skills are also important, as mathematicians must be able to interact with others, including nonmathematicians, and discuss proposed solutions to problems.

Statistics

About 147 colleges and universities offer degrees in statistics. Required subjects for statistics majors include mathematics through differential and integral calculus, statistical methods, mathematical modeling, and probability theory. Additional courses that undergraduates should take include linear algebra design and analysis of experiments, applied multivariate analysis, and mathematical statistics. Because computers are used extensively for statistical applications, a strong background in computer science is highly recommended. For positions involving quality and productivity improvement, training in engineering or physical science is useful. A background in biological or health science is important for positions involving the preparation and testing of pharmaceutical or agricultural products. For many jobs in market research, business analysis, and forecasting, courses in economics and business administration are helpful.

A bachelor's degree with a major in statistics or mathematics is the minimum requirement for the statistics field. Teaching and research positions require a graduate degree, often a doctorate, in statistics.

Operations Research

With more than 130 colleges and universities offering programs or courses in operations research management science, decision sciences, and related fields, academia is another promising area.

The following is a partial list of colleges and universities that offer four-year degree programs in computer science, mathematics, and operations research.

ALABAMA

Alabama Agricultural and Mechanical University
Normal, 35762

Alabama State University
Montgomery, 36101

Alexander City State Junior College
Alexander City, 35010

Auburn University
Auburn University, 36849

Birmingham-Southern College
Birmingham, 35254

Chattahoochee Valley State Community College
Phenix City, 36869

Gadsden State Community College
Gadsden, 35902–0227

Huntingdon College
Montgomery, 36106

Jacksonville State University
Jacksonville, 36265

Livingston University
Livingston, 35470

Mobile College
Mobile, 36613

Samford University
Birmingham, 35229

Selma University
Selma, 36701

Spring Hill College
Mobile, 36608

Stillman College
Tuscaloosa, 35403

University of Alabama
  Tuscaloosa, 35487–6132

University of North Alabama
  Florence, 35632

University of South Alabama
  Mobile, 36688

ALASKA

University of Alaska at Anchorage
  Anchorage, 99699

University of Alaska at Fairbanks
  Fairbanks, 99201

ARIZONA

Arizona State University
  Tempe, 85287

Central Arizona College
  Coolidge, 85228

North Arizona University
  Flagstaff, 86011

University of Arizona
  Tucson, 85721

ARKANSAS

Arkansas State University
  State University, 72467

Harding University
  Searcy, 72143

Henderson State University
  Arkadelphia, 71923

University of Arkansas
  Fayetteville, 72701

CALIFORNIA

California Institute of Technology
Pasadena, 91125

California State University
Los Angeles, 90032

College of Notre Dame
Belmont, 94002

National University
San Diego, 92108

Pepperdine University
Malibu, 90265

San Diego State University
San Diego, 92182

San Francisco State University
San Francisco, 94132

Stanford University
Stanford, 94305

University of California
Berkeley, 94720

University of San Diego
San Diego, 92110–2492

Whittier College
Whittier, 90608

COLORADO

Colorado State University
Fort Collins, 80523

Mesa State College
Grand Junction, 81502

University of Colorado
Denver, 80217

CONNECTICUT

Central Connecticut State University
New Britain, 06050

Fairfield University
Fairfield, 06430

Southern Connecticut State University
New Haven, 06515

University of Connecticut
Storrs, 06269

University of Hartford
West Hartford, 06117

Yale University
New Haven, 06520

DELAWARE

Delaware State College
Dover, 19901

University of Delaware
Newark, 19716

DISTRICT OF COLUMBIA

American University
Washington, DC 20016

Georgetown University
Washington, DC 20057

University of the District of Columbia
Washington, DC 20008

FLORIDA

Daytona Beach Community College
Daytona Beach, 32115

Edison Community College
   Fort Myers, 33906–6210

Florida Institute of Technology
   Melbourne, 32901

Florida State University
   Tallahassee, 32306

Tampa College
   Tampa, 33614

University of Central Florida
   Orlando, 32816

University of Miami
   Coral Gables, 33124

GEORGIA

Albany State College
   Albany, 31705

Emory University
   Atlanta, 30322

Gainesville College
   Gainesville, 30503

Georgia Institute of Technology
   Atlanta, 30332

University of Georgia
   Athens, 30314

HAWAII

University of Hawaii
   Hilo, 96720

IDAHO

Boise State University
   Boise, 83725

University of Idaho
  Moscow, 83843

ILLINOIS

Bradley University
  Peoria, 61625

DePaul University
  Chicago, 60605

Illinois Institute of Technology
  Chicago, 60616

Knox College
  Galesburg, 61401

Northeastern Illinois University
  Chicago, 60625

Northern Illinois University
  DeKalb, 60115

Northwestern University
  Evanston, 60628

Roosevelt University
  Chicago, 60505

Southern Illinois University
  Carbondale, 62901

University of Illinois
  Urbana-Champaign, 61820

INDIANA

Indiana State University
  Terre Haute, 47809

Purdue University
  West Lafayette, 47907

University of Evansville
  Evansville, 47722

University of Notre Dame
 Notre Dame, 46556

Valparaiso University
 Valparaiso, 46383

IOWA

Drake University
 Des Moines, 50311

Grinnell College
 Grinnell, 50112

Northwestern College
 Orange City, 51051

University of Dubuque
 Dubuque, 52001

University of Iowa
 Iowa City, 52242

KANSAS

Kansas State University
 Manhattan, 66506

Ottawa University
 Ottawa, 66067

University of Kansas
 Lawrence, 66045

KENTUCKY

Georgetown College
 Georgetown, 40324

Kentucky State University
 Frankfort, 40601

Murray State University
 Murray, 42071

University of Kentucky
  Lexington, 40506–0032

University of Louisville
  Louisville, 40292

LOUISIANA

Louisiana State University
  Shreveport, 71115

Tulane University
  New Orleans, 70118

University of New Orleans
  New Orleans, 70148

MARYLAND

College of Notre Dame of Maryland
  Baltimore, 21210

U.S. Naval Academy
  Annapolis, 21402

University of Maryland
  Baltimore, 21201

MASSACHUSETTS

Boston College
  Chestnut Hill, 02167

Boston University
  Boston, 02254

Harvard University
  Cambridge, 02138

MICHIGAN

Eastern Michigan University
  Ypsilanti, 48197

Kalamazoo College
  Kalamazoo, 49007

University of Michigan
  Ann Arbor, 48109

Wayne State University
  Detroit, 48202

MINNESOTA

Concordia College
  Moorhead, 56562

University of Minnesota
  Duluth, 55812

MISSISSIPPI

University of Mississippi
  University, 38677

MISSOURI

Missouri Southern State College
  Joplin, 64801

MONTANA

Montana State University
  Bozeman, 59717

NEBRASKA

Peru State College
  Peru, 68421

NEVADA

University of Nevada
  Las Vegas, 89154

Western Nevada Community College
Carson City, 89703

NEW HAMPSHIRE

University of New Hampshire
Durham, 03824

NEW JERSEY

Princeton University
Princeton, 08544

Trenton State College
Trenton, 08650–4700

NEW MEXICO

College of Santa Fe
Santa Fe, 87501

NEW YORK

Brooklyn College
New York, 11210

Columbia College
New York, 10027

Cornell University
Ithaca, 14853

New York University
New York, 10011

NORTH CAROLINA

Duke University
Durham, 27706

Queens College
Charlotte, 28274

NORTH DAKOTA

University of North Dakota
  Grand Forks, 58202

OHIO

Ohio State University
  Columbus, 43210

University of Toledo
  Toledo, 43606

OKLAHOMA

Oklahoma State University
  Stillwater, 74078

OREGON

Oregon State University
  Corvallis, 97331

PENNSYLVANIA

University of Pennsylvania
  Philadelphia, 19104

University of Scranton
  Scranton, 18510–4501

WASHINGTON

Washington State University
  Pullman, 99164

WEST VIRGINIA

Bethany College
  Bethany, 26032

WORKING ENVIRONMENT

Computer scientists and others with careers in this general field work in offices or laboratories. In crunch times more than the usual forty-hour week may be required.

Because computer scientists and systems analysts spend long periods of time in front of a computer terminal typing on a keyboard, they are susceptible to eyestrain, back discomfort, and hand and wrist problems.

Computer and mathematics professionals may work alone, in a small group, or as an integral part of a team that includes engineers, computer scientists, physicists, technicians, and others. Deadlines, overtime work, special requests for information or analysis, and travel to attend seminars or conferences may be part of the job.

EMPLOYMENT

About 666,000 individuals work as computer scientists and systems analysts. Although they are found in most industries, the greatest concentration is in computer and data processing service firms. Many others work for government agencies, manufacturers of computer and related electronic equipment, insurance companies, and universities.

A substantial number work as consultants and are hired to work specified periods of time to complete a particular project; perhaps a few months or even a year or two.

Over 73 percent of mathematicians work for the government or industry. About 16,000 individuals work as mathematicians with another 16,000 holding mathematics faculty positions in colleges and universities. Most nonfaculty mathematicians work in the government and in service and manufacturing industries. The Department of Defense is the primary federal employer of mathematicians; more than three-fourth of the mathematicians employed by the federal government work for the navy, army, or air force. A significant number of mathematicians also work in state governments. In the private sector, major employers within service industries include research and testing services and computer and data processing services. In manufacturing, the aircraft, chemicals, computer, communications, machinery, electrical equipment, and office equipment industries are key employers.

There are about 16,000 statisticians. About one-fourth work for the federal government, most likely the Departments of Commerce (especially the Bureau of the Census), Agriculture, and Health and Human Services. Most of the remaining jobs are in private industry, especially in the insurance, transportation equipment, research and testing services, management and public relations, and computer and data processing services industries. Others work in colleges and universities and for business and professional organizations.

Opportunities for promotion are best for those statisticians with advanced degrees. Master's and Ph.D. degree holders enjoy greater independence in their work, and are qualified to engage in research, to develop statistical methodology, or, after several years of experience in a particular area of technological application, to be statistical consultants.

Operations research analysts, employed in most industries, number about 50,000. Of the 13,000 members of the Institute for Operations Research and the Management Sciences (INFORMS), approximately 33 percent work in private industry, 56 percent in academia, and 9 percent in government and military jobs. Major employers include computer and data processing services, commercial banks and savings institutions, insurance agencies, engineering and management services firms, manufacturers of transportation equipment, airlines, and the federal government. Some analysts work for management consulting agencies that conduct operations research for firms that do not have an in-house operations research staff.

Most analysts in the federal government work for the armed forces. In addition many operations research analysts who work in private industry perform work that is directly or indirectly related to national defense.

Job Prospects

The *Occupational Outlook Handbook* reports that computer scientists and systems analysts will be among the fastest growing occupations through the year 2005. This demand is a result of the fact that most organizations wish to maximize the efficiency of their computer systems. As international and domestic competition increases, organizations will face growing pressure to use technological advances in areas such as office and factory automation, telecommunications, technology, and scientific research. Computer scientists and engineers will be needed to develop this new technology. In addition the complexity associated with designing new applications is growing. More computer scientists will be needed to develop innovative and increasingly sophisticated systems.

Employment of mathematicians is expected to increase more slowly than the average for all occupations through the year 2005. Many firms engaged in civilian research and development that use mathematicians are not planning to expand their research departments much, and in some cases may reduce them. Expected reductions in defense-related research and development will also affect their employment, especially in the federal government.

Organizations are increasingly using operations research and management science techniques to improve productivity and quality and to reduce costs. Those seeking employment as operations research or management science analysts who hold a master's or Ph.D. degree should find good opportunities through the year 2005. The field is expected to grow much faster than the average for all occupations.

The *Occupational Outlook Handbook* reports that although employment of statisticians is expected to grow more slowly than the average for all occupations through the year 2005, job opportunities should remain favorable. Many statistics majors, particularly at the bachelor's degree level, but also at the master's degree level, may find positions in which they do not have the title of statistician. This is especially true for those involved in analyzing and interpreting data from other disciplines such as economics, biological science, psychology, or engineering.

Federal governmental agencies will need statisticians in fields such as agriculture, demographic consumer and producer surveys, transportation, Social Security, health, education, energy conservation, and environmental quality control. Private industry, in the face of increasing competition and strong government regulation, will continue to require statisticians, especially at the master's and Ph.D. degree levels, to not only monitor but improve productivity and quality in the manufacture of various products including pharmaceuticals, motor vehicles, chemicals, and food products. For example, pharmaceutical firms will need more statisticians to assess the safety and effectiveness of the rapidly expanding number of drugs.

Statisticians with knowledge of engineering and the physical sciences will find jobs in research and development working with scientists and engineers to help improve design and production processes in order to ensure consistent quality of newly developed products.

PROFESSIONAL ASSOCIATIONS

The Operations Research Society of America has about 7,500 members. The Institute of Management Sciences has more than 8,000 members from academia, business, and government. These organizations publish journals and other materials. They conduct workshops and forums on advances in operations research. Members use the society to keep up with developments in the field and to meet others in the profession.

The largest group to represent the interests of statisticians is the American Statistical Association with more than 15,000 members. The Institute of Mathematical Statistics fosters work in the mathematical theory of probability and has a membership of 3,500 members.

The American Mathematical Society has 28,500 individual members and 485 institutions. The Society for Industrial and Applied Mathematics fosters the application of mathematics to problems in industry and science.

SALARIES

Computer designers, computer product design engineers, and software designers generally earn between $30,000 and $50,000 annually. The United States Department of Labor reports median annual earnings of systems analysts at about $42,000 (ranges from $25,000 to $60,000).

According to a College Placement Council survey, starting salary offers for mathematics graduates with a bachelor's degree average about $28,400 a year, master's degrees $33,600, and new doctoral graduates $41,000. Starting salaries are generally higher in industry and government than in educational institutions. For example, the American Mathematical Society reports that median annual earnings for new recipients of doctorates in research are $30,200; for those in teaching or teaching and research (nine-ten month academic year), $34,000; for those in government, $53,000; and for those in business and industry, $53,000.

In the federal government, the average annual salary for mathematicians in supervisory, nonsupervisory, and managerial positions is $43,232, and for mathematical statisticians, $54,109.

Operations research analysts with a master's degree generally earn about $30,000 to $35,000 per year. Experienced operations research analysts may expect to earn about $50,000, and top individuals could earn more than $90,000. Recent surveys indicate an average salary of $65,000 to $85,000 per year in business and industry; $57,500 in federal government for those with at least a master's degree. Associate professors (doctorate level) earn about $60,000 per year.

The average annual salary for operations research analysts in the federal government in nonsupervisory, supervisory, and managerial positions is about $58,000.

The average annual salary for statisticians in the federal government in nonsupervisory, supervisory, and managerial positions is about $52,000; mathematical statisticians average about $55,000. In the private sector experienced statisticians may top earnings of $100,000 to $150,000 per year.

FOR ADDITIONAL INFORMATION

American Mathematical Society
P.O. Box 6428
Providence, RI 02940

American Society for Information Science
8720 Georgia Avenue
Silver Spring, MD 20910-3602

American Statistical Association
1429 Duke Street
Alexandra, VA 22314

Association for Systems Management
1433 West Bagley Road
Cleveland, OH 44138

Association for Women in Computing
P.O. Box 21100
St. Paul, MN 55123

Association for Women in Mathematics
Box 178
Wellesley College
Wellesley, MA 02181

Conference Board of the Mathematical Sciences
1529 Eighteenth Street, NW
Washington DC 20036

Institute for the Certification of Computer Professionals
2200 East Devon Avenue, Suite 268
Des Plaines, IL 60018

The Institute of Management Sciences
290 Westminster Street
Providence, RI 02903

Institute of Mathematical Statistics
3401 Investment Boulevard, No 7
Hayward, CA 94545

Institute for Operations Research and the Management Sciences
290 Westminster Street
Providence, RI 02903-3432

Mathematical Association of America
1529 Eighteenth Street NW
Washington, DC 20036

Military Operations Research Society
101 South Whiting Street, Suite 202
Alexandria, VA 22304

National Systems Programmers Association
4811 South 76th Street
Milwaukee, WI 53220

The Operations Research Society of America
1314 Guilford Avenue
Baltimore, MD 21202

Society for Industrial and Applied Mathematics
3600 University City Science Center
Philadelphia, PA 19104-2688

CHAPTER 7

THE SOCIAL SCIENCES

If you know you are on the right track, if you have this inner knowledge, then nobody can turn you off... regardless of what they say.

—Barbara McClintock, in Evelyn Fox Keller, "Barbara McClintock: The Overlooked Genius of Genetics," *A Passion To Know: 20 Profiles in Science* (1985)

The range of professions that falls beneath the heading *social sciences* is vast and varied, yet the common denominator among the individual professions is that each field offers a particular perspective on our society as a whole or on a select segment of our social organization. In order to examine society from the required perspective of a particular social science profession, practitioners rely heavily on research techniques to gain an understanding of past and present situations and to prepare for future changes and events.

Social scientists study all aspects of human society, from the distribution of goods and services, to the beliefs of newly formed religious groups, to modern mass transportation systems. Social science research seeks to uncover patterns and identify problems in an attempt to provide insights that help us understand the different ways in which individuals and groups make decisions, exercise power, or respond to change. Through their studies and analyses, social scientists and urban planners assist educators, government officials, business leaders, and others in solving social, economic, and environmental problems. Ultimately their aim is to provide the information needed to alleviate human suffering and promote social welfare.

Social sciences are interdisciplinary in nature. Specialists in one field often find that the research they are performing overlaps work that is being conducted in another social science discipline. Regardless of their field of specialization, social scientists are concerned with some aspect of society, culture, or personality.

The following is a partial list, arranged alphabetically, of the fields belonging to the broad category of social sciences:

anthropology
economics
geography
history
marketing research
political science
psychology
public policy
social work
sociology
urban and regional planning

Research is at the very core of what social scientists do. In the process, they use established or newly discovered methods to compile facts and theories that add to the body of human knowledge that already exists. Applied research is usually designed to produce information that will allow individuals to make wiser decisions or manage their lives more efficiently.

The process of research is sometimes called the scientific method. It consists of the following steps:

1. Stating the problem or posing a question.
2. Designing the study.

3. Collecting the data.
4. Processing the data.
5. Analyzing the data.
6. Interpreting the findings.
7. Writing the research report.

Although each of the social science disciplines is dependent on accumulated information, the research techniques for gathering the necessary data are dictated by both the inherent characteristics of the profession and by the individual requirements of a project. A well-conducted research program, regardless of the profession it is serving, begins with a clear design created to feasibly and economically generate the data for the prespecified purposes and intended uses of the results. The program design not only embraces the objectives of the project, but it also takes into consideration the constraints of budget, time, geographical area, and staff availability.

In her book, *Research Design, Strategies and Choices in the Designing of Social Research,* Catherine Hakim gives a thorough description of many research techniques employed to gather data. The various methods may either be used exclusively or in conjunction with one another. Below is a partial list:

- Reviewing literature and preexisting studies in a secondary analysis of the material to meet the new objectives.
- Qualitative research from explorative, free-form interviews and/or group discussions to gain descriptive reports and individual perceptions, attitudes, or behaviors.
- Analysis of the factual matter contained within administrative records and documents from various public or private organizations.
- Sampling of a representative population with questionnaires, and then applying statistics to the sample to extrapolate for the entire population.

- In-depth case studies of individuals, social groups, or organizations, usually preselected and conducted over a long period of time.
- Regular surveying of a population, either repeated at regular intervals or conducted continuously, yielding a breadth of information and indicating changes within the population.

Data collection may take many other forms including living and working among the people; analysis of historical records; archaeological and other field investigations; experiments with human subjects or animals in a psychological laboratory; preparation of maps and other graphic materials; and administration of questionnaires and standardized tests.

SOCIOLOGISTS

There are some differences in research techniques among the various social science disciplines. Sociologists usually conduct surveys, employ various interviewing techniques, or engage in direct observation to gather data. For example, after providing for controlled conditions, an organizational sociologist might test the effects of different styles of leadership on individuals in a small work group. A medical sociologist might study the effects of terminal illness on the family as a whole.

Sociological researchers also evaluate the efficacy of different kinds of social programs. They might examine and evaluate specific programs such as income assistance, job training, health care, or remedial education. These professionals extensively use statistics and computer techniques in their research, along with qualitative methods such as focus group research and social impact assessment. They study issues related to abortion rights, AIDS, high school dropouts, homelessness, and latchkey children. Sociologists often work closely with community groups and members of other professions, including psychologists, physicians, economists, statisticians, urban and regional planners, political scientists, anthropologists, law enforcement personnel, criminal justice officials, and social workers.

PSYCHOLOGISTS

Research psychologists investigate the physical, cognitive, emotional, or social aspects of human behavior. They rely almost exclusively on results gained from scientific experiments. Psychologists in applied fields counsel and conduct training programs, do market research, apply psychological treatments to a variety of medical and surgical conditions, or provide mental health services in hospitals, clinics, or private settings.

Like other social scientists, psychologists formulate hypotheses and collect data to test their validity. They may gather information through controlled laboratory experiments; personality, performance, aptitude, and intelligence tests, observations, interviews, and questionnaires; clinical studies; or surveys. Computers are widely used to record and analyze this information.

ECONOMISTS

Economists base evaluations on secondary analysis of existing research. Their work might focus on topics such as energy costs, inflation, interest rates, farm prices, rents, imports, or employment. Those who are primarily theoreticians may use mathematical models to develop theories on the causes of business cycles and inflation or the effects of unemployment and tax legislation.

Depending on the topic under study, economists devise methods and procedures for obtaining the data they need. For example, sampling techniques may be used to conduct a survey, and econometric modeling techniques may be used to develop forecasts. Preparing reports usually is an important part of the economist's job. He or she may be called upon to review and analyze the relevant data, prepare tables and charts, and write up the results in clear, concise language. Being able to present economic and statistical concepts in a meaningful way is particularly important for economists whose research is policy directed.

MARKETING RESEARCH ANALYSTS

Marketing research analysts provide information that is used to identify marketing opportunities; to generate, refine, and evaluate marketing actions; and to monitor marketing performance. Like economists, marketing research analysts devise methods and procedures for obtaining the information they need. They often design surveys and questionnaires; conduct telephone, personal, or mail interviews; and sometimes offer product samples to assess consumer preferences and indicate current trends. Once the data are compiled, they code, tabulate, and evaluate them. Based on the results, they make recommendations to management. They also conduct public opinion research polls to familiarize the media, government, lobbyists, and others with the needs and attitudes of the public.

Analysis of the data resulting from a research project often is the responsibility of individuals other than those conducting the research. The information, once analyzed and presented in a comprehensible format, is then used by professionals to evaluate the effectiveness of social programs, social policies, or the activities of particular agencies or organizations; it also can be used to aid in the decision of whether to implement any variety of social reforms.

THE ALAN GUTTMACHER INSTITUTE

Many existing social service organizations perform a multitude of services, one of which is to conduct research. An example of this is the

New York–based Alan Guttmacher Institute, a Corporation for Reproductive Health Research, Policy Analysis and Public Education. The institute was named to honor a distinguished and dedicated obstetrician-gynecologist, author, and leader in reproductive rights. Dr. Guttmacher, during his presidency of the Planned Parenthood Federation of America in the late 1960s and early 1970s, saw the need for the institution that now bears his name and encouraged and nurtured its development. AGI was incorporated as an independent, not-for-profit organization in 1977. To achieve its goals, the institute undertakes research as needed; publishes its own and others' relevant, scientifically rigorous research data; and uses this information as the basis for targeted, action-oriented outreach activities. Throughout its work, the institute pursues a conscious integration of research and action so that each is enriched and reinforced by the other. AGI provides reliable, balanced, nonpartisan information on sexual activity, contraception, abortion, and childbearing. This involved—and has involved for more than two decades—a commitment to identifying key questions, collecting and analyzing data to answer them, and publishing the answers. It entails mining government data for new findings, surveying individuals, and making sense of and reaching new audiences with research results. It also means conducting interviews with the media, testifying before federal and state legislative bodies, and responding to the information requests of groups and individuals.

Careers in research and development within the social sciences can come from the private or public sector and may be organization or project specific. The trend today is toward large-scale, jointly funded, multidisciplinary research programs. These projects require professionals and workers at all levels and often span long periods of time and more than one geographic location. In a word, this modern trend creates opportunities for individuals seeking a career in one of the social sciences.

Meet Robin Bates

Robin Bates is an assistant professor at the Jane Addams College of Social Work, University of Illinois, Chicago Campus. She has an M.S.W. from the University of Washington and a Ph.D. in social welfare from the University of Washington.

"For me, the turning point occurred when I was working on a research project dealing with the court system and children in state foster care. My findings ended up changing the way the court operated. And I thought that was really cool—I realized I could make a difference. How exhilarating! So I started to do research on existing programs and practices to determine what could be done to change the system. As a result of this endeavor, I enrolled as a Ph.D. student because I came to know that Ph.D. credentials would allow me to more easily explore research topics that interested me.

"In my present position as an assistant professor, teaching is my primary responsibility. That means that I spend a considerable amount of time preparing class work, grading papers, talking to students, or working on developing a new course. The other part of my time is devoted to research and other school responsibilities. Since I teach policy courses, I attend a large number of policy meetings in the community. I also serve in a number of other capacities: on an advisory board, on a Senate Research Committee, and on several university committees.

"One of the nice things about working in a university setting is that you can pursue your individual research interests by setting up projects that will explore topics that appeal to you. My field of interest is women in the criminal justice system or juveniles at risk of being part of the criminal justice system or have been part of the system. For instance, I just presented a paper in Las Vegas on battered women in prison who have killed the man who abused them.

"Exactly what does it mean to be involved in research projects? What you are doing depends on what point you are at in the project. At the beginning you are developing the project and writing a grant to secure the money you need to fund it. Once a project is decided, you set up the data collection, which is either using existing data from a database or developing an instrument to collect original data. It usually takes quite a long time between developing an instrument and developing a methodology of how the project will be done. Then the project is implemented, the results are recorded, and the report is written. The next stage is trying to get it published or presenting it at conferences. I'm usually involved in three to five projects at a time, so I could be negotiating the very beginning of a project at the same time that I'm writing up the results on another and analyzing the data on a third. There are so many interesting things to participate in and learn about, it's often difficult to decide which to take on. On the one hand I feel I have a great deal of autonomy, and on the other I always feel pressure because I have so many things that I have to get done. This translates to a typical work-week between sixty and eighty hours.

"In some cases people may think, 'I'll get a Ph.D., become a college professor, and it'll be really fun.' What you should know is that you will have research responsibilities and you really need to enjoy doing this kind of work. More and more universities (at least in the social sciences), are requiring people to have good research skills and the ability to obtain outside funding to complete research projects. Sometimes it's a shock, particularly in social work, to realize that in order to become able researchers, you will be required to learn statistics and develop methodological skills.

"Having a university position takes much more self discipline than many other careers because a lot of productivity is expected, excellent teaching skills are expected, good research skills and output are expected, and participation in other areas is expected. And class preparation time is much more than you ever think it's going to be. However, while it is true that high school teachers get paid more than college teachers, virtually everyone is here because this is where we all want to be."

EDUCATION AND TRAINING

High school students need to follow a college preparatory curriculum. This includes: history, speech, language, mathematics, English, social science, social studies, history, math, and computer science.

A bachelor's degree in the social sciences consists of classroom instruction in social work practice, social welfare policies, human behavior and social environment, and social research, along with 400 hours of supervised fieldwork.

Training in statistics and mathematics is essential for most social scientists. Mathematical and other quantitative research methods are increasingly used in economics, geography, political science, experimental psychology, and other fields. The ability to use computers for research purposes is mandatory in most disciplines.

To get a master's degree, students must complete two more years of special instruction, some of which must be in the form of an internship. During the internship most students prepare for a specialty, such as child welfare. In some schools students can elect to study a field of case work, group work, or administrative work.

Educational attainment of social scientists is among the highest of all occupations. The Ph.D. or equivalent degree is a minimum requirement for most positions in colleges and universities and is important for advancement to many top-level nonacademic research and administrative posts. Doctoral degrees usually require up to four years of additional study beyond the master's degree.

Sociology

About 860 schools offer bachelor's degree programs, about 150 schools offer master's degree programs, and approximately 190 colleges and universities offer doctoral degree programs.

Core requirements for sociology degrees include courses in statistics, research methodology, and sociological theory. Other courses cover a wide range of topics such as aging (gerontology), criminal justice, delinquency, deviance and social control, family and society, gender roles, social psychology, rural sociology, organizational behavior and analysis, mental health, and science and technology.

A master's degree in sociology is usually the minimum requirement for employment in applied research or community college teaching. For sociologists, the Ph.D. degree is essential for most senior level positions in research institutes, consulting firms, corporations, and government agencies, and is required for appointment to permanent teaching and research positions in colleges and universities. Sociologists holding a master's degree can qualify for administrative and research positions in public agencies and private businesses. Training in research, statistics, and computer methods is an advantage in obtaining such positions.

In the federal government, candidates generally need a college degree with twenty-four semester hours in sociology, including course work in theory and methods of social research.

Certification by the Sociological Practice Association (SPA) is required for some positions in clinical sociology and applied sociology, especially at the doctoral level. Candidates for certification must have at least one year of relevant experience, an advanced degree from an accredited school, and demonstrate competence at SPA-sponsored workshops and conferences.

Psychologists

Psychologists with a Ph.D. qualify for a wide range of teaching, research, clinical, and counseling positions in universities, elementary and secondary schools, private industry, and government. Persons with master's degrees in psychology can administer tests as psychological assistants. Under the supervision of doctoral-level psychologists, they can conduct research in laboratories, conduct psychological evaluations, or perform administrative duties.

In most cases two years of full-time graduate study are needed to earn a master's degree in psychology. Requirements usually include practical experience in an applied setting or a master's thesis based on a research project. Five to seven years of graduate work are usually required for a doctoral degree. The Ph.D. degree culminates in a dissertation based upon original research. Courses in quantitative research methods, which include the use of computers, are an integral part of graduate study and usually necessary to complete the dissertation.

Economists and Market Researchers

Potential economists and marketing research analysts can gain experience gathering and analyzing data, conducting interviews or surveys, and writing reports on their findings while in college. This experience can prove invaluable later in obtaining a full-time position in the field, since much of their work in the beginning centers around these duties. With further experience, economists and marketing research analysts eventually are assigned their own research projects.

Graduate training increasingly is required for many economist and marketing research analyst jobs and for advancement to more responsible positions. Marketing research analysts may earn a master's degree in business administration, marketing, statistics, or some related discipline. Some schools help graduate students find internships or part-time employment in government agencies, economic consulting firms, financial institutions, or marketing research firms. Like undergraduate students, work experience and contacts can be useful in testing career preferences and learning about the job market for economists and marketing research analysts.

Persons considering careers as economists or marketing research analysts should be able to work accurately with detail since much time is spent on data analysis. Patience and persistence are necessary qualities since economists and marketing research analysts may spend long hours on independent study and problem solving. Marketing research analysts particularly must be able to work well with others since they often interview a wide variety of people.

Objectivity, openmindedness, and systematic work habits are important in all kinds of social science research. Written and oral communication skills are essential for all social scientists. An ability to get along with others, emotional maturity, objectivity, and sensitivity are all positive traits for those in this profession.

WORKING ENVIRONMENT

Most social scientists have regular hours. Generally working behind a desk, either alone or in collaboration with other social scientists, they read and write research reports. Many experience the pressures of deadlines and tight schedules, and sometimes they must work overtime, for which they are generally not reimbursed. Since social scientists often work as an integral part of a research team, their routine may be interrupted frequently by telephone calls, letters to answer, special requests for information, meetings, or conferences. Travel may be necessary to collect information or attend meetings. Social scientists on foreign assignment must adjust to unfamiliar cultures and climates.

Some social scientists do fieldwork. For example, anthropologists, archaeologists, and geographers often must travel to remote areas, live among the people they study, and stay for long periods at the site of their investigations. They may work under primitive conditions, and their work may involve strenuous physical exertion.

Social scientists employed by colleges and universities generally have flexible work schedules, often dividing their time among teaching, research, consulting, or administrative responsibilities.

Sociologists in the federal government work primarily for the Departments of Health and Human Services, Agriculture, Education, Commerce (Bureau of the Census), Defense, and the General Accounting Office. They may also work in special government agencies such as the Peace Corps, National Institutes of Health, the National Institute of Aging, the World Bank, the United Nations, and the World Health Organization.

EMPLOYMENT

There are about 258,000 social scientists. Over half are psychologists; over one-third of all social scientists are self-employed and are involved in counseling, consulting, or research.

Social scientists work for a wide range of employers. Forty percent work for federal, state, and local governments; 30 percent work in health, research, and management services firms; and 20 percent work in educational institutions as researchers, administrators, and counselors. Other employers include social service agencies, international organizations, associations, museums, historical societies, computer and data processing firms, and business firms.

Sociologists in the federal government work primarily for the Departments of Health and Human Services, Agriculture, Education, Commerce (Bureau of the Census), Defense, and the General Accounting Office.

Career opportunities are most favorable in large cities, for example, New York City, Washington DC, and Chicago.

Job Prospects

Employment of social scientists is expected to grow faster than the average for all occupations through the year 2005, spurred by rising concern over the environment, crime, communicable disease, mental illness, the growing elderly and homeless populations, the increasingly competitive global economy, and a wide range of other issues. Psychology, the largest social science occupation, is expected to grow much faster than average. Economists and marketing research analysts, urban and regional planners, and all other social scientists combined, including anthropologists, geographers, historians, politician scientists, and sociologists, should experience average growth.

Additional positions for sociologists will stem from the increasing demand for research in various fields such as demography, criminology, gerontology, and medical sociology and the need to evaluate and administer programs designed to cope with social and welfare problems. Growing recognition of the research and statistical skills of sociologists and the role they can play in solving a wide range of problems in business and industry may spur more job growth.

Demand for marketing research analysts should be particularly strong due to an increasingly competitive global economy. Marketing research provides organizations valuable feedback from purchasers, allowing companies to evaluate consumer satisfaction and more effectively plan for the future.

PROFESSIONAL ASSOCIATIONS

Voluntary certification is offered by the National Association of Social Workers (NASW), which grants the title ACSW (Academy of Certified Social Workers) or ACBSW (Academy of Certified Baccalaureate Social Workers) to those who qualify.

The American Marketing Association (AMA) has more than 52,000 members. This group fosters research; sponsors seminars, conferences, and student marketing clubs; and offers a placement service. The Marketing Research Association (MRA) has a membership of more than 2,200 companies and individuals including research companies, data collection companies, and users of research. It publishes a newsletter, a marketing research business series, and an annual *Research Service Directory.*

SALARIES

Social scientists earn an average of $37,000. According to a recent survey by the College Placement Council, bachelor's degree holders received starting offers of about $19,000, master's about $29,000, and doctoral social scientists, $30,000. The average salary of all social scientists working for the federal government in nonsupervisory, supervisory, and managerial positions is about $43,000.

According to the American Psychological Association, the median annual salary of psychologists with a doctoral degree is $50,000 in research positions.

Social workers in administration, teaching, research, and private practice earn more than most other social workers.

The average annual salary for all sociologists in the federal government in nonsupervisory, supervisory, and managerial positions is about $54,000.

FOR ADDITIONAL INFORMATION

The Alan Guttmacher Institute
120 Wall Street
New York, NY 10005

The American Anthropological Association
4350 North Fairfax Drive, Suite 640
Arlington, VA 22203

American Association for State and Local History
530 Church Street, 6th Floor
Nashville, TN 37219

American Marketing Association
250 South Wacker Drive, Suite 200
Chicago, IL 60606

American Political Science Association
1527 New Hampshire Avenue NW
Washington, DC 20036

American Sociological Association
1722 N Street NW
Washington, DC 20036

Archeological Institute of America
675 Commonwealth Avenue
Boston, MA 02215

Association of American Geographers
1710 Sixteenth Street NW
Washington, DC 20009

Council of American Survey Research Organizations
3 Upper Devon
Port Jefferson, NY 11777

Marketing Research Association
2189 Silas Deane Highway, Suite 5
Rocky Hill, CT 06067

National Association of Social Workers
750 First Street NE, Suite 700
Washington, DC 20002-4241

National Network for Social Work Managers, Inc.
6501 North Federal Highway, Suite 5
Boca Raton, FL 33487

Population Association of America
1722 N Street NW
Washington, DC 20036

Society for American Archaeology
900 Second Street NE, #12
Washington, DC 20002

Sociological Practice Association
Department of Pediatrics/Human Development
B240 Life Sciences
Michigan State University
East Lansing, MI 48824-1317

CHAPTER 8

SCIENCE RESEARCH TECHNICIANS

A good scientist is a person in whom the childhood quality of perennial curiosity lingers on. Once he gets an answer, he has other questions.

—Frederick Seitz, *Fortune* (April 1976)

WANTED: Chemical technicians who thrive on change. Must enjoy working in new and challenging areas such as materials science, biotechnology, and polymers. Skills required:

1. Setting up and conducting chemical bench experiments.
2. Operating or monitoring production processes.
3. Operating and maintaining laboratory and analytical instruments.

NEEDED: Capacity to understand how industry and jobs are changing and to adapt to new conditions. Sound technical and interpersonal skills are necessary.

Working under the supervision of area-specific scientists, science technicians (also known as laboratory technicians, research technicians, or research and development technicians) solve problems in research and development and investigate, invent, and help improve products by implementing the use of the theories and principles of science in conjunction with mathematics. In a more practical role than scientists, technicians make extensive use of computers, computer-interfaced equipment, robotics, and high-technology industrial applications such as biological engineering.

Once the scientists develop the theories and set up the research projects, the laboratory technicians are usually responsible for getting the work done—often for industrial chemicals, plastics, synthetic fibers, food preservatives, paints, and pharmaceutical companies—by conducting tests; setting up, operating, and maintaining laboratory instruments; preparing chemical solutions; monitoring experiments; calculating and recording results; and often developing conclusions. Following are several categories of science research technicians:

Agricultural technicians. These technicians work with agricultural scientists in food and fiber research, production, and processing. Some conduct tests and experiments to improve the yield and quality of crops or to increase the resistance of plants and animals to disease, insects, or other hazards.

Biological technicians. These technicians work with biologists studying living organisms. They may assist scientists who conduct medical research, helping to find a cure for cancer or AIDS, for example, or they may help conduct pharmaceutical research. Biological technicians also analyze organic substances such as blood, food, and drugs; some examine evidence in criminal investigations. Biological technicians working in biotechnology labs use the knowledge and techniques gained from basic research by scientists, including gene splicing and recombinant DNA, and apply these techniques in product development.

Chemical technicians. These technicians work with chemists and chemical engineers developing and using chemicals and related products and equipment. Most do research and development, testing, or other laboratory work. For example, they might test packaging for design, materials, and environmental acceptability; assemble and operate new equipment to develop new products; monitor product quality; or develop new production techniques. Those who focus on basic research might produce compounds through complex organic synthesis.

When the testing is completed and the results are tabulated, the technician submits the data to chemists for review. Together they examine the project to determine if they need to build new or improved formulations for an existing product. Finally they submit their written reports to management personnel who will then make any necessary decisions based upon the research results.

Nuclear technicians. These technicians operate nuclear test and research equipment, monitor radiation, and assist nuclear engineers and physicists in research.

Petroleum technicians. These technicians measure and record physical and geologic conditions in oil or gas wells using instruments lowered into wells or by analysis of the mud from wells.

EDUCATION AND TRAINING

Anyone desiring to follow a career as a science technician should take as many high school science and math courses as possible. This should include algebra, trigonometry, geometry, chemistry, physics, biology, and any other laboratory courses. A good background in English is beneficial because laboratory technicians must have strong writing and speaking skills. Also helpful are industrial arts, mechanical drawing, and social studies classes.

Though there are a number of routes to becoming a science technician, most science technicians usually train for at least two years in programs especially geared for the type of work they will be performing. A focus on laboratory-oriented course work is advantageous. Many junior or community colleges offer associate degrees in a specific technology or a more general education in science and mathematics. For example, the chemical laboratory technician program usually includes courses in general chemistry, quantitative and instrumental analysis, physics, mathematics, organic laboratory equipment and procedures, and technical report writing.

A number of two-year associate-degree programs are designed to provide easy transfer to a four-year college or university. Often science technicians have a bachelor's degree in science or mathematics, or they at least have taken a number of science and mathematics courses in four-year colleges or universities. Technical institutes usually offer technician training, but it typically includes less theory and general education than junior or community colleges. The armed forces offers certain types of training. In some cases on-the-job training is available.

Since the computer is such an important part of the daily work of a science technician, those training for this career should develop strong computer skills. Also important are communications skills and the ability to get along with others. Both are necessary to perform tasks properly.

In some cases licensing or certification may be needed. For example, chemical laboratory technicians who work with food products, such as milk or dairy products, may be required to have a state or local license.

WORKING ENVIRONMENT

Science technicians may work in varied settings including the outdoors or indoors, in laboratories, in remote locations, or in offices. Usually they have regular working hours. In some cases they are exposed to hazardous chemicals and conditions. For example, chemical technicians often work with toxic chemicals, nuclear technicians may be exposed to radiation, and biological technicians occasionally come in contact with radioactive materials or disease-causing organisms.

EMPLOYMENT

There are about 250,000 science technicians. About 40 percent are employed by manufacturing concerns (mostly in the chemical industries), but others work for the petroleum refining and food processing industries. About 20 percent work in colleges and universities and another 12 percent for research and testing services.

The federal government employs about 19,000 technicians, primarily placed in the Departments of Agriculture, Commerce, Defense, and the Interior.

Job Prospects

In a positive vein, employment opportunities for science technicians are expected to increase about as fast as the average for all occupations through the year 2005. The outlook for chemical and biological technicians looks especially promising.

PROFESSIONAL ASSOCIATIONS

The American Chemical Society provides a variety of services to its members (and also to nonmembers). For a current list of schools offering programs in chemical technology, write to the American Chemical Society (listed at the end of the chapter).

SALARIES

The average salary for science technicians is about $25,000, but some individuals are earning closer to $50,000 in this field.

Biological science technicians employed by the federal government in nonsupervisory, supervisory, and managerial positions average about $25,000; mathematical technicians average about $30,000; physical science technicians average about $32,000; and meteorological technicians average about $37,000.

FOR ADDITIONAL INFORMATION

American Chemical Society
    Education Division, Career Publications
    1155 Sixteenth Street, NW
    Washington, DC 20036

American Institute of Biological Sciences
    730 Eleventh Street, NW
    Washington, DC 20001

Barron's Guide to the Two-Year Colleges will have information regarding programs for those interested in becoming science technicians.